The End of Development?

Third World in Global Politics
Series Editor: Dr Ray Bush (University of Leeds)

The Third World in Global Politics series examines the character of politics and economic transformation in the global South. It does so by interrogating contemporary theory and practice of policy makers, planners and academics. It offers a radical and innovative insight into theories of development and country case study analysis. The series illustrates the importance of analysing the character of economic and political internationalisation of capital and national strategies of capital accumulation in the global South. It highlights the political, social and class forces that are shaped by internationalisation of capital and which in turn help shape the character of uneven and combined capitalist development in the South. The series questions neo-liberal theories of development and modernisation and in highlighting the poverty of the mainstream offers critical insight into the theoretical perspectives that help explain global injustice and the political and social forces that are available across the globe providing alternatives to economic and political orthodoxy of the advocates of globalisation.

The End of Development?

Modernity, Post-Modernity and Development

Trevor Parfitt

Pluto Press

LONDON • STERLING, VIRGINIA

First published 2002 by Pluto Press
345 Archway Road, London N6 5AA
and 22883 Quicksilver Drive,
Sterling, VA 20166–2012, USA

www.plutobooks.com

ISBN 0 7453 1638 7 hardback
ISBN 0 7453 1637 9 paperback

British Library Cataloguing in Publication Data
A catalogue record for this book is available from the British Library

Library of Congress Cataloging in Publication Data
Parfitt, Trevor W., 1954–
   The end of development? : modernity, post-modernity and development /
Trevor Parfitt.
     p. cm.
   ISBN 0–7453–1638–7
   1. Development economics. I. Title.
    HD75 .P376 2002
    306.3—dc21
                                                         2001005311

10   9   8   7   6   5   4   3   2   1

Designed and produced for Pluto Press by
Chase Publishing Services, Fortescue, Sidmouth EX10 9QG
Typeset from disk by Stanford DTP Services, Towcester
Printed in the European Union by Antony Rowe, Chippenham, England

IN MEMORIAM

Anthony Ivers (1946–96)
Stephen Riley (1949–99)

Friends and peers who instinctively understood
about being for the other

Contents

Acknowledgements

In undertaking this project I have accumulated numerous debts to those who have helped and supported me in various ways. Thanks are due to the American University in Cairo, which supported my research with time off and financial assistance. Many of my colleagues at AUC were helpful. Dr Dan Tschirgi and Dr Tony Lang were encouraging about early drafts of my manuscript, whilst Dr Kate McInturff, and Dr Mark Salter made useful suggestions about later drafts. Josh Stacher was of great help in researching material concerning Islamism. I am also grateful to Ray Bush who encouraged me at every stage of this project. Both Ray and Pandeli Glavanis took time to read various drafts and make useful comments for which I thank them. I am particularly grateful to Ms Pamela Ritchie for her dedication and skill in preparing my manuscript for the publisher. My thanks to all the staff at Pluto Press who have helped me throughout this project. Last, but not least, I thank my sister Patricia who afforded me hospitality at various points in the production of this book. Needless to say, any shortcomings or errors are my responsibility alone.

1   Introduction: The End of Development?

Towards the end of the 1980s a crisis emerged in development theory. Initially, this was referred to as the 'impasse'. Most of the traditional theories that were used to examine and delineate development were regarded as having fallen into doubt (e.g. modernisation theory, the various forms of underdevelopment theory and more recently neo-liberalism). Leftist strategies of development were at least partially, if not wholly discredited by the collapse of communism, whilst theories that advocated a development path based on the Western capitalist model were also seen as having delivered few if any of the benefits that they had seemed to promise. Many parts of the 'Third World' had been struggling under the weight of accumulated debts to the industrialised countries for more than a decade, while also attempting to apply the market-influenced Structural Adjustment Programmes that had been forced on them by the West, in particular the Washington institutions, the World Bank and the International Monetary Fund (IMF). Structural adjustment was supposed to create the conditions for economic growth in the Third World by removing obstacles to the efficient operation of the free market. By the end of the 1980s (indeed up to the present day) there was (and still is) little evidence that the ubiquitous Structural Adjustment Programmes (SAPs) had stimulated any growth, or created conditions conducive to growth. Under these circumstances it was hardly surprising that many of those involved in development began to feel that the old theories had failed (a notable exception included those practitioners and academics who were associated with the Washington, and other aid institutions, that had made a considerable intellectual and financial investment in such strategies as SAPs). The question was where to go from that position. Such was the nature of the 'impasse'.

In the absence of any trustworthy theoretical grounding many theorists have sought a path through the impasse by reference to the body of theory variously known as 'post-modernism', or poststructuralism. Post-modernism is associated with a wide body of theory by analysts as various as Jean Baudrillard, Jean Francois Lyotard, Emmanuel Levinas, Michel Foucault, Jacques Derrida, and Fredric Jameson. Although post-modernism is notoriously difficult to define, it is possible to point to certain themes, or tendencies, that are associated with this type of thinking (post-modernity is too diffuse to refer to it as a school of thought). In particular, post-modernists tend to take a critical position with regard to the habits of thought associated with modernity (although, as we shall see, some of them are more sympathetic than others to the body of ideas that is usually associated with modernity). Aspects of modern thinking that are often subjected to post-modern critique include the belief that history incorporates a teleology of progress, that if one examines human history one can detect a process of progress towards greater levels of civilisation, or towards human emancipation. Classical Marxist theory would represent one example of such a teleological theory, in that human society is seen as progressing from one socio-economic stage of development to another more advanced one, the culmination of this process being achieved with the establishment of communism, the most advanced form of society, and the goal of history. Post-modern theorists would deny that such a dynamic of progress is built into history, and would reject the possibility that there could be such a thing as the goal of history. History is viewed simply as a contingent succession of events. Post-modernists would also tend to criticise what is often viewed as a peculiarly modernist faith in the ability of humankind to improve their conditions through science, broadly conceived as the ability to mould and shape their world through the application of technology and such methods as rational techniques of planning. This is not to say that post-modernists argue that technology and planning never result in the desired, or at least beneficial outcomes, although some come quite close to such a position at times (e.g. Paul Feyerabend on science). However, they are usually suspicious of the ability of planners and social engineers to achieve their supposedly benign objectives for society (and this is to leave aside the possibility that they may express such benign objectives as a cover for less generally beneficial aims).

The above does not amount to anything like a full definition of post-modernism. However, it does indicate that certain problems arise out of post-modernism for the related concepts of development and aid. After all, most, if not all of the traditional development theories, whether of the left or the right, took the form of teleological theories that envisaged development in terms of achievement of some sort of societal end goal, such as communism in the case of the former group, or capitalism in the case of the latter. Postmodernists would not only dismiss leftist theorists who saw history as a progress towards communism, but also pro-capitalist theories, such as that of Rostow, who argued that all societies progressed through five stages of development, culminating in the achievement of high mass consumerism on the American model. It also follows from the above observations that post-modernists would be critical of the whole enterprise of development planning, both at the macro-level of national and regional planning, and at the micro-level of designing specific project interventions, such as an agricultural, health or educational project. Indeed, there are plenty of examples of development plans and projects that misfire for a variety of reasons, including poor design, failure to anticipate operational or other problems, bureaucratic inefficiency or lack of capacity and so forth. Given the plenitude of such evidence and the post-modern suspicion of teleology and planning, it is hardly surprising that the theorists who took a post-modern route out of the impasse often ended by taking a rejectionist position towards development.

One of the first examples of this post-development line of thinking was *The Development Dictionary*, published in 1992. Its editor, Wolfgang Sachs debunked development in the following terms:

> The idea of development stands like a ruin in the intellectual landscape. Delusion and disappointment, failures and crimes have been the steady companions of development and they tell a common story: it did not work. Moreover, the historical conditions which catapulted the idea into prominence have vanished: development has become outdated. But above all, the hopes and desires that made the idea fly, are now exhausted: development has grown obsolete. (Sachs, 1992: 1)

In the same volume, Gustavo Esteva provides a powerful critique of the word 'development' examining its origins as a Western concept and the way in which it has been used by imperial powers of various stripes as a support for their own ideological projects of domination. He also notes the changing content of the word, as it has moved from denoting an essentially economic process of growth to take on other connotations such as participation and human-centred development (Esteva, in Sachs, 1992: 6–25). Sachs comments that 'development has become an amoeba-like concept, shapeless but ineradicable', with 'contours so blurred it denotes nothing ...' (Sachs, 1992: 4).

This renders it eminently clear that as far as the authors are concerned the whole enterprise of development should be abandoned as having done far more harm than good. Over the next few years *The Development Dictionary* was joined by a number of other volumes that variously used elements of post-modern theory to critique, and often to reject the idea of development. Arturo Escobar used critical techniques associated with Michel Foucault to analyse and dismiss development as a discourse in *Encountering Development: The Making and Unmaking of the Third World* published in 1995. Discourse may be defined as referring to bodies of ideas and concepts, or theory, which mediate power through their effects upon the way we act (this is a rather simplistic definition, but discourse will be dealt with in greater detail in future chapters). The same year saw the publication of the reader edited by Jonathan Crush, *Power of Development*, which gathered together a number of articles (including an excerpt from Escobar's book) that took a similar approach to the analysis of development. M.P. Cowen and R.W. Shenton also used techniques influenced by Foucault to trace the history of development as an idea in *Doctrines of Development* (1996), although they take a more nuanced approach of criticising what they see as the negative and repressive content of the concept of development in the hope of liberating it for a more progressive and emancipatory reading. Majid Rahnema and Victoria Bawtree edited *The Post-Development Reader* (1997), in which they gathered a variety of readings that were critical of aspects of development. In his afterword Rahnema used elements of Foucauldian thought together with aspects of Ghandian and Confucian thinking to argue for the rejection of development. Esteva, together with Madhu Suri Prakash, produced *Grassroots Post-Modernism: Remaking the Soil of Cultures* (1998), which argued once again that development had done more harm than good, and that emancipation of the world's social majorities (so-called because the majority of the world's population are those living at the grass roots in the Third World, although there are concentrations of the poor in the North) is best left to movements originating with those social majorities (a position similar to that put by Escobar). Numerous periodical articles and other publications could be cited that take a similar line. It would seem that we have a new 'post-development' school of thought, or discourse, emerging, which coheres around the central contentions that development has been harmful, and that consequently it should be consigned to the dustbin of history in order to make way for new strategies of emancipation associated with what are sometimes referred to as 'new social movements' originating in the 'Third World', such as the Zapatistas of Mexico.

This is a line of thought that many find persuasive given the plentiful evidence of the ill effects that can be attributed to development initiatives in many countries, and the evident bankruptcy of so many of the theories that have been used to justify development. There is also much persuasive analysis in the above-mentioned volumes and associated post-development writings. Cowen and Shenton's analysis of the concept of development is undeniably scholarly and cogent, revealing much about the body of ideas that have fed into the genesis of development as a discourse. Similarly, Escobar's critique of neo-liberal development theory (particularly that underlying the aforementioned SAPs) is trenchant, while Esteva and Prakash provide some convincing arguments against development policies predicated on human rights. One could point to other instances of worthwhile analysis associated with post-development thinking.

However, the point of this book is that the author fundamentally disagrees with some of the main contentions of this line of thought. This book will argue that the post-development school's call for the end of development is misconceived and precipitate and that its view as to what should follow development raises problems that can be more effectively solved within the context of a pro-development approach. It is hoped that this book will make a contribution towards the elaboration of such an approach.

What then is wrong with post-development thinking? In the first instance it is worth observing that although many post-development thinkers have made use of post-modern analysis, they have not always used it particularly effectively, and they do not appear to have read very widely. The majority of the above-mentioned authors have tended to use the body of theory developed by Michel Foucault. However, as we shall see, their use of his theory is incomplete in the sense that they focus on techniques of analysis that he developed in his earlier works, and they have failed to take on board all the nuances that Foucault later added to these methods. Further, they have failed to address some significant critiques of Foucault's methodology by such commentators as Jurgen Habermas. In addition there are many other post-modern or critical thinkers whose ideas could have been examined such as Jacques Derrida and Emanuel Levinas (whose ideas will be considered in Chapter 4 of this book). One might also have expected a little more attention to be paid to the work of Habermas, whose position as a prominent critic of post-modernity should have alerted post-development analysts to the fact that there are alternative positions to the ones that they have embraced. A central argument running through this book will be that a more thorough reading of some of these alternatives leads to quite different conclusions than those asserted by the post-development theorists.

For example, a common position in poststructuralist theory holds that the meaning of any word, or signifier, will be characterised by slippage from one context to the next. However, as we have seen, Sachs and Esteva point out such slippage in the meaning of the word 'development' only as an occasion for derision. This book will argue that any worthwhile definition of development will necessarily be unstable. Furthermore, it will argue for a conception of development that is centrally concerned with emancipation. In this sense development may be considered as entailing achievement of the freedom of a community, nation, or group, to pursue its own projects for realisation of a good life on the proviso that it does the least possible harm to others. Such a definition can never be finalised inasmuch as it connotes a wide variety of actual and possible projects. We shall also use the work of Jacques Derrida to argue that any attempt at presenting a complete definition is bound to fail since it will inevitably omit and repress projects that may legitimately be identified as falling within the ambit of development.

This implies that existing attempts to provide complete definitions of development are likely to be exclusory and therefore repressive. Some may be deliberately repressive as in the case of movements that premise one group's development as being dependent on exclusion of another group. Others may be more open being concerned with the emancipation of the social majorities in the Third World. This reading of the development discourse is suggestive that the word is a vigorously contested one. Indeed, various interests compete to move this discourse in the directions that they respectively favour, some of which might be deemed conservative in that they involve various forms of closure, whilst others are more emancipatory. This contestation is not suggestive that development is redundant, or in any sense a fit subject for ridicule.

Rather, it is indicative that development is a contested ground. To be sure, when conservative forces manage to gain control of the development agenda the results for the social majorities are often deleterious, as when the British Conservative Government of the 1980s used its aid budget to fund projects such as the notorious Pergau Dam in Malaysia (which was condemned as being ecologically and socially harmful, as well as cost inefficient) on the proviso that the Malaysian Government would buy British arms. However, the converse of this is that progressive forces can campaign to prevent such abuses and to move the development agenda in more inclusive directions. The contention of this book is that there is more to be gained by doing precisely that rather than taking a rejectionist position like the post-development theorists.

Those who subscribe to a post-development position would tend to retort that progressive initiatives are certain to be coopted by conservative forces and turned against the interests of the social majorities. Alternatively, they would argue that the development discourse is itself based on Western ideas of progress and therefore cannot help but take the form of an imposition of those ideas on the South, thus repressing local cultures and interests. With regard to the first point, it seems likely that conservative groups will try to gain control of progressive initiatives, and in many instances they may succeed – but does that invalidate the efforts of progressive forces to gain control of the development agenda? To the extent that their efforts result in activities that are beneficial to those at the grass roots, surely not (on the proviso that the judgement of what is beneficial is made by those at the grass roots rather than by a bureaucrat from the aid agency). The second argument has more complex ramifications in that it suggests that the development discourse cannot help but be imperialist because it represents an imposition of the power of one set of interests, what Esteva and Prakash refer to as the social minorities (largely, though not exclusively, concentrated in the North), over another set of interests, the social majorities. However, as we shall see, it can equally be argued that all discourses can be seen as impositions of power by one interest over another. Moreover, the outcome of such an act of power need not necessarily be wholly deleterious for those subjected to that act. It could actually have beneficial effects. This line of argument is suggestive that it is pointless to reject development for being implicated with the application of power. Rather, it is indicative once again that interests associated with the social majorities should endeavour to exert their power effectively to move the development agenda in progressive directions that will benefit and empower the social majorities.

It can also be argued that objective conditions in the Third World demand an active effort to ensure that the development discourse is won for the progressive agenda. There is much evidence to suggest that the majority of people in the 'Third World' are experiencing deteriorating living conditions. Escobar notes this, pointing out that statistics on growing hunger, the 'Third World debt crisis, and destruction of the rain forest are all likely to be used to promote the view that aid and development are necessary' (1995: 213). He would wish to resist such a conclusion given that he analyses development as a discourse of power that is used to the detriment of the social majorities. However, if we accept the above arguments that the agenda set by the development discourse can be moved in an emancipatory direction, Escobar's argument falls. His fears that a strengthened development discourse will be bad for the social majorities would be borne out to the extent that development policy is dominated by those who wish to exploit the Third World. But this is not an inevitable outcome. The need to prevent such an outcome makes it all the more urgent to exert pressure to ensure that an emancipatory direction is taken. Indeed, it could be argued that a moral impetus is active here directing those forces sympathetic to the social majorities to actively campaign for a progressive development discourse. It would be immoral for the North to evade its responsibility to assist the social majorities at a time when their living conditions are deteriorating, in some cases to the point where life can no longer be supported.

This leads us to one of the difficulties raised by the post-development scenario of emancipation led by the new social movements, which is in essence an ethical problem. We have already observed that an integral element of the post-development scenario (for most though not all of the analysts mentioned above) is that the North should cease intervening in the affairs of the social majorities through its development policies. One might ask if this leaves any acceptable role for the North in a post-development Third World, or if any intervention is to be seen as interference? As we shall see, post-development thinkers seem undecided on this and no clear position has emerged. This question becomes even more complex if we pose it in terms of intervention by the social minorities rather than by the North. After all, many of the post-development thinkers are members of the social minorities even if they have originated in the Third World. They work in Western universities, and many of them have worked in aid organisations. Yet they clearly feel that their intervention is justified. At the risk of presumption, one suspects that they feel an obligation to intervene in the attempt to help those who can be seen to be in need of assistance. A central contention of this book is that members of the social minorities are ethically obliged to assist the social majorities. However, it is clear that not all forms of such intervention would be acceptable. The post-development thinkers are correct to note that many of the interventions that have taken place under the rubric of development have been repressive and disruptive of local societies and cultures. In future chapters we shall argue that there are ethically acceptable models for provision of assistance available within the development discourse.

An ethical problem also arises with the post-development school's entrustment of the emancipatory project to the new social movements. This category covers a wide variety of groupings and organisations emanating from the grass roots of the Third World, ranging through the Chipko Movement to preserve the forest in Bangladesh, the Zapatistas of Mexico, Sendero Luminoso in Peru, and the various Islamist movements operating in many parts of the Middle East. Are we to take a relativist position in which the products and characteristics of each culture are regarded as equally legitimate and consequently argue that all of these movements are legitimate representatives of emancipation in their respective areas of the world? Most of the post-development thinkers give a very clear negative answer to this contention. Some are to be accepted as genuinely emancipatory movements while others are not. For example, Esteva and Prakash embrace the Zapatistas as a genuine post-development emancipatory movement, but reject any claims that Islamic fundamentalist movements might have to such a status. Their reasons for such a decision are never clearly explained. This is a serious oversight. Clearly, we are all likely to feel that some movements or causes are worthy of our support. It may be that their objectives seem so meritorious that we feel a moral compulsion to offer our support to them. Equally, there will be some organisations that we feel unable to support, indeed, their objectives may seem so undesirable that we feel obliged to oppose them. The crucial issue here is the reasoning underlying our decision. In considering the process of how we reach such decisions we must have reference to another common position in post-modern thinking to the effect that we are all perspectival. This means that we are only able to think from within our own perspectives, each of which is characterised by its own normative biases and cultural, or other values. Consequently, each of us is biased and what seems right and justifiable to one may seem pernicious and wrong to another. The hostility to Islamic fundamentalism displayed by Esteva and Prakash may well seem like an unreasonable prejudice to an observer from the Muslim world. In deciding which causes we support as legitimate and which ones we reject as harmful, or misguided, we are obliged to explain ourselves. It seems inevitable to this author that such explanations will have an ethical dimension given that they deal in classifying what is right, in the sense of being worthy of support, and what is wrong, or undeserving of support. Given that we are operating across cultural boundaries this is complicated because we are dealing with different perspectives that have different ideas of what is right and what is wrong. This suggests that we must have reference to an ethics that is universal and that is not founded within a particular cultural tradition with its partial biases. In future chapters we shall examine the possibility for such an ethics. It will be argued that certain elements of post-modern and critical thought, particularly that associated with Derrida and Levinas, provide the basis for such an approach that will enable us to make distinctions between the new social movements.

To summarise, the central purpose of this book is to reject the calls for the end of development, and to utilise post-modern and critical theory to demonstrate that there can after all be forms of development that are complementary to the emancipatory projects of the new social movements. The character of this development would be guided by an ethics based on the deconstructive thinking of Derrida, which is in turn influenced by the ethical philosophy of Levinas.

The argument of the book will be organised as follows. Chapter 2 will initially examine some central themes in post-modern thinking, particularly inasmuch as they have a bearing on the post-development debate. It will then pass on to a more detailed consideration of the post-development literature, demonstrating that it has imported certain problems from post-modern thought, notably that of relativism. In Chapter 3, we shall proceed to an examination of some of the post-modern and critical literature that has been employed in post-development thought. Firstly, the work of Foucault will be examined to demonstrate some of the problems in his work that have been ignored by such commentators as Escobar and Rahnema.

A consideration of the critique addressed to Foucault by Habermas will lead to an analysis of the latter's work to assess what light it may shed on questions pertaining to development. Chapter 4 will focus on the work of Derrida and Levinas, explicating various attempts to synthesise Derrida's technique of deconstruction with the Levinasian view of ethics. This chapter will culminate in a consideration of how a deconstructionist ethics might be applied in a political context. In Chapter 5 we shall examine a number of the new social movements, applying the 'ethical/deconstructive' approach outlined in Chapter 4 to them. Chapter 6 will apply this viewpoint to aid policy and its application, raising the questions as to what forms of development aid actually assist in the emancipation of the social majorities and are ethically acceptable, with a view to indicating the direction that a viable development policy might take in the future.

2 From Post-Modernity to Post-Development

2.1 INTRODUCTION

In this chapter we shall initially examine some of the central issues associated with post-modern thought. This analysis will not constitute an attempt to provide a complete definition, or account of post-modernity. It is, in any case, dubious whether one could produce a wholly satisfactory account of such a diffuse and complex (the less sympathetic would say woolly) body of thought. The main emphasis of this summary of post-modernism will be to highlight those issues that have relevance for development/post-development theory. As noted in the Introduction, certain aspects of post-modern thought have been incorporated into post-development theory without sufficient attention being paid to the complexity of these ideas. Some of these post-modern ideas are the subject of fierce debate because they are viewed in some quarters as causing severe problems for the possibility of developing any coherent body of theory for explaining the world – that is, for distinguishing what is true from what is false, or for determining what is good and what is bad. In other words, such critics would accuse post-modernism of being characterised by an extreme relativism, amounting to nihilism. To the extent that this criticism sticks it has radical implications. Adherence to a nihilist position would mean that we could not generate any explanatory structure through which we could make truthful claims about reality. It follows from this that we would also lack the ability to distinguish one set of ideas from another in terms of their accuracy in describing the world, or of their ethical position. For example, we would be unable to develop an argument that Marxist theory explains the capitalist system any better than neo-liberal theory, or vice versa. We could not claim with any authority that a democratic system of governance is superior to a fascist system. Similarly, Esteva and Prakash would have no basis for arguing that their post-development agenda is better than any development strategy, or that the Zapatistas represent an emancipatory grass-roots movement while Sendero Luminoso do not.

Clearly, if the post-development theorists have unconsciously imported such problems into their collective work then considerable doubt is cast on its value or utility. It is for this reason that in the first part of this chapter we shall examine post-modern thought, placing an emphasis on the development of such controversies as that over relativism. The second part of the chapter will then analyse post-development thinking with a view to establishing how post-modern ideas have been incorporated into it and how far the problems associated with post-modernity have left any imprint on it.

2.2   FROM MODERNITY TO POST-MODERNITY

Post-modern thought has emerged at least in part as a response to some of the perceived problems of modernity. For that reason, we must start by briefly examining the emergence of modernity, with particular emphasis on some of the ideas that post-modern thinkers found problematic. Although the emergence of modernity is often associated with the Enlightenment period, and particularly with the late eighteenth century, in fact the complex of ideas that we associate with modernity developed over a long period, arguably lasting at least two millennia. It is for this reason that we must very briefly survey the pattern of ideas in the classical era so that we may trace (albeit with extremely broad brushstrokes) how the various elements of modernism developed out of them.

The philosophers of the classical age regarded nature as a unitary whole that was divine in its own right. Humankind and, for that matter, the gods were all regarded as part of the natural order, which set the rules of conduct for both gods and mortals. The Greek concept of 'kosmos' encapsulated physical nature and moral and aesthetic values into an ordered, unified whole. Also included in this category was the 'logos', which made the rule of nature intelligible to man. Louis Dupré defines the logos as 'the rational foundation that normatively rules all aspects of the cosmic development' (Dupré, 1993: 17). Because the human mind was seen as part of nature and the laws of nature were made self-evident by the logos, humankind did not need to experience any sense of doubt about whether or not it properly apprehended the nature of reality. To quote Dupré once again 'both mind and reality participated in the same intelligibility' (1993: 17) produced by the logos. Reality was unproblematic and accessible to humanity under this system of ideas. It can be seen that knowledge of reality was founded on the logos, which was conceived as part of the kosmos. To put it another way, it was through the logos that humankind had the assurance that it could obtain true knowledge of reality. It was the foundation for human knowledge.

Gradually, over a period of centuries, this organic view of nature began to break down. An initial crack in the intellectual edifice appeared with the Judaeo-Christian conception of a God who had created the cosmos out of nothing, and who therefore had to be considered as separate from the cosmos. However, God was still considered to be present in the world, not least through the life of Christ, who was regarded as a human incarnation of the logos. Thus, God came to be the guarantor of human ability to attain true knowledge. Through the embrace of God humankind could obtain access to universal truths. Religious philosophers such as Thomas Aquinas proposed that, since nature was God's creation, empirical investigation of the natural world was a key to obtaining universal truth. As Tarnas notes:

> Aquinas repeatedly quoted from Paul's Letter to the Romans, 'the invisible things of God are clearly seen...by the things that are made'. The divine invisibles ... could be approached only through the empirical, the observation of the visible and particular. By experiencing the particular through the senses, the human mind could then move toward the universal, which made intelligible the particular. (1991: 182)

The problem was that empirical investigation often produced results that were in conflict with various aspects of religious belief. The most obvious example was the Copernican revolution, which held that the Earth moved around the Sun in contradiction to several passages in the scriptures that referred to the earth as unmoving (Tarnas, 1991: 252). That such inconsistency between the findings of science and religious precepts was a problem even prior to Copernicus is indicated by the fact that the fourteenth-century scholar, William of Ockham, denied that humans could gain access to God's universal truths through empirical investigation. Ockham's position was that since God was all-powerful he was not limited by human rationality or by nature, which were merely particular creations among the infinity of creativity of which God was capable. Therefore, humankind could not establish universal truths through the study of nature, and the only truths humans were capable of establishing were those that could be attained through empirical investigation of the natural world. Although Ockham's main concern was to protect the inviolability of religious belief, it can be seen that two crucial implications of his work were that nature was stripped of any divine significance, and humankind was restricted to scientific investigation of the natural world. This gave an impetus to the growing importance of science, which was reflected in the work of such figures as Francis Bacon and Robert Boyle. The desacralisation of nature also gave rise to a viewpoint that was strongly endorsed by Bacon, and others such as Descartes, that nature could be mastered and moulded for human benefit through the application of science. However, Ockham had also put the foundation of human knowledge into question. If God did not guarantee that his universal truth was reflected in nature, how was one to obtain truthful knowledge? The burden of this task was now transferred to the individual investigator.

The growing uncertainty concerning how to found knowledge was reflected in a growth of philosophical scepticism. Philosophers such as Montaigne noted that there were classical precedents to point out that there was a difference between reality and appearances, that the senses could be misleading, and that human belief was at least partially shaped by custom, all of which led him to suspect that no absolute truth could be established. Such views influenced Descartes, who tried to establish secure foundations for knowledge by using doubt as the basis for his methodology. Anything that was subject to doubt could not be accepted as the truth. Even things that we directly experience could be the result of some illusion and are therefore subject to some doubt. However, what we can be sure of is that we have to exist in order to experience doubt or anything else. Hence his dictum *cogito ergo sum* – 'I think therefore I am'. The one thing that each of us can be certain of is that s/he exists. In this way Descartes established a foundation for knowledge in the cogito, or the thinking subject. In doing so he originated one of the fundamental precepts of modern philosophy. As Tarnas aptly puts it:

> Here, then, was the prototypical declaration of the modern self, established as a fully separate, self-defining entity, for whom its own self-awareness was absolutely primary – doubting everything except itself, setting itself in opposition not only to traditional authorities but to the world, as subject against object, as a thinking, observing, measuring, manipulating being, fully distinct from an objective God and an external nature. (1991: 280)

True knowledge was no longer to be founded by nature, or by God, but by the rational subject.

However, there was still the problem of how to establish the truth of anything beyond the cogito given the questionable reliability of our senses. The thinking subject may know that s/he exists, but how can s/he establish the truth of anything in the outside world? In order to solve this problem Descartes argued that a good and truthful God would not seek to mislead humankind in its attempts to gain knowledge through its use of the faculty of reason. Consequently, we could obtain knowledge of the real world in the faith that God would not have shaped the world in such a way as to mislead us. However, there were problems with this formulation. Descartes emphasised the distinction between the idea that we have of some object and the reality of that object in the external world. This raises a doubt as to how far the idea that we have developed of the object actually corresponds to its reality. Dupré points out that Descartes' method of proving the existence of God tends to exacerbate this doubt. Descartes had argued that the thought of God is so perfect that it would be beyond the capacity of an imperfect human thinker unless the thought had proceeded from a cause in reality, this being the actual existence of God. Dupré quotes one such argument in Descartes' Third Meditation as follows:

But in order for a given idea to contain such and such objective reality [in other words, ideal reality as a mode of thought], it must surely derive it from some cause which contains at least as much formal reality [in other words, the reality of actual existence] as there is objective reality in the idea. (Dupré, 1993: 82)

Dupré goes on to comment on this passage:

In this argument for the existence of God, 'objective' stands for 'representational', and significantly, representation is conceived as being so independent of whatever it represents that no extra-mental reality may correspond to it at all – only a real cause of the idea is required. At that point the question how the world we know in our ideas relates to the real world becomes a critical one. (1993: 82)

In other words, our idea of God may proceed from the cause that God actually exists, but the idea we have of God may not resemble the actuality of God in any way. If we apply this principle to other objects that we perceive in reality, it follows that our idea of these objects may be quite different from their reality. This would suggest that the foundation of knowledge in the cogito is unreliable. This leaves a very substantial foothold for sceptical critiques of Descartes' attempt to found knowledge in the cogito, or the subject.

Kant attempted to solve this problem by founding knowledge completely within the autonomous rational subject, without having recourse to any external guarantees from God, or any other power. He accepted the force of the scepticist kernel of doubt that what we thought we perceived accorded with reality, but he also wanted to defend the gains for knowledge that were being achieved by scientists such as Newton. In his solution of this problem, he proposed that humankind is only able to experience the world by virtue of the fact that the human mind is structured by certain types of *a priori* knowledge (that is, knowledge that is prior to experience, or empirical justification). Humans must have knowledge of space and time in order to experience anything at all. Additionally they need *a priori* knowledge of such concepts as substance, causality, quantity, and relation. If our experience of the world was not mediated through such categories, it would be completely disorganised and have no meaning for us. It follows that such concepts must already structure our minds in order for us to have any meaningful experiences at all. The faculty of reason is then applied to the raw data of experience in order to make sense of it, deduce findings, and apply order to our world. Thus, scientists are able to gather data, analyse it, construct theories of gravitation and so forth. Human knowledge is thus founded on the application of reason to our experience of the world.

It may be noted that this represents an important departure in the enterprise of identifying foundations for our knowledge. Prior to Kant, knowledge had been founded by relation to some external authority, whether it was nature (the logos), or God. It could be argued that Descartes had made the initial move away from this tendency by founding knowledge in the cogito, but even he had to have recourse to a benevolent God, who ensured that the cosmos was not structured in a deliberately misleading way (as we have seen, there were problems with this idea). However, for Kant, knowledge was founded completely within the reasoning subject. This had radical implications. Given that Kant accepted that all our experience of the world is mediated through our senses, and organised by our minds in accordance with our *a priori* knowledge of concepts like causation, he accepted that we do not gather knowledge of external reality, or as he put it, 'the world in itself', at all. He held that we apply order to our reality through the application of reason, asserting that reason 'commands' nature, it 'legislates', framing 'for itself with perfect spontaneity an order of its own according to ideas, to which it adapts the empirical conditions' (in Pippin, 1991: 55). This is a fundamental departure from the idea that man attains knowledge of an independent reality through the grace of God. In Kant's view humankind shapes reality in accordance with reason. Although sceptics might argue that this means we know nothing of reality in itself, Kant could reply that the way in which our mental structures (that is, our *a priori* knowledge of such categories as causation and so forth) process our experience of that world, and the application of our reason to that experience, all enable us to construct analyses, and to draw conclusions that work for us in the real world. For example, Newton's theory of gravity can be seen to work, and humans can confidently make plans on the basis that it will continue to work. Consequently, we do not need to worry that we do not have knowledge of the world in itself. Rationality provides sufficient grounding for our knowledge to work.

However, Pippin argues that there is still room for sceptical doubts of such a foundation. He notes that the Kantian position that we have no access to immediately accessible experience of the real world makes it essential that our *a priori* knowledge should not distort the raw data that our senses perceive. Pippin continues:

> If experience in some fundamental way underdetermines the basic conceptual classifications with which experience is finally discriminated, and if 'pure reason' cannot determine 'objectively', independently of experience, such conceptual constraints, is Kant not on the verge of replacing reason with the imagination, of, de facto, poeticizing the origin of our most fundamental classifications, or rendering them 'groundless' rather than 'self-grounded'? (Pippin, 1991: 56-7)

In other words, if experience is not in some sense properly processed by the *a priori* categories (the basic conceptual classifications), and reason is not able to check this, either by itself, or by having recourse to experience, Kant's foundation for knowledge is thrown into doubt. Pippin also cites Fichte's critique that 'the Kantian appeal to reason' may be 'ungrounded unless we could show how such a commitment could be viewed as the "product" of a subject's purely self-determining, or absolutely free activity' (Pippin, 1991: 57). It is by no means automatic that people have recourse to reason even concerning decisions or problems that are vital to them. Consequently, Kant's foundation of knowledge in reason is vulnerable to the sceptical position.

Having traced the debate on truth and its foundations up to the time of Kant, and the Enlightenment era, it may be observed that we have touched on a number of the central aspects of modernity. One element clearly is the emphasis given to establishing foundations for knowledge, which also tends to be associated with a faith in the adequacy of reason for investigating and explaining the world. We have also seen that the unity of humankind and the gods within nature broke down with the encroachment of modernity. As it became clear that the empirical investigations of early science were producing results that were contradictory to the scriptures, it became necessary to insulate the Christian faith from these contradictions of its tenets. Consequently, God came to be conceived as an all-powerful deity, remote from nature, which was merely one of His creations rather than being a divinity in its own right. This desanctification of nature (or 'disenchantment of the world', to use Weberian terms) prepared the way for the thoroughly modern view that it was entirely proper to use science to mould nature in accordance with human needs and desires. The increasing remoteness of the divine led people to start placing more faith in the ability of science to improve their lot in this life, rather than focusing on the hope that a distant ineffable deity would rescue them in the next one.

Another important factor in the emergence of modernity was the changing status of humankind. The ancient Greeks regarded humankind as a part of nature, but gradually this changed and one of the central themes of modernity emerged – the autonomy of the free individual. Humanity as a mass became differentiated into individual subjects, each one thinking and reasoning for himself or herself. Given that humanity was no longer seen as being organically linked to nature, the world, inclusive of other people, became related to each subject as an object. It is also worth observing that the status Kant allocated to reason placed the reasoning subject in the role of shaper and organiser of nature. Not only did he mean that the human mind organised its sensory impressions of the world into an understandable order for the thinking subject, but also that the subject used reason to mould nature (considered as an object) into an order in accordance with his or her desires. This conception of the relationship between humanity and nature was thoroughly complementary to the established view that humankind could use science (this being one of the central manifestations of reason) to exploit nature for its own benefit. Indeed, the cumulative achievements of science at the time of the Enlightenment seemed conducive to the view that here was the key that could unlock the mysteries of nature to humankind's benefit.

This Enlightenment faith in the benefits of science, combined with the high value attached to the autonomy, or the freedom of the individual, led to an upsurge of what has been termed 'grand theory', or metatheory. In the Introduction we noted that a feature common to much modernist theory is that it incorporates a teleology of progress. Such theories as Marxism view the history of human society as being characterised by a dialectical dynamic, which forces society to move through a series of progressive stages until humankind is emancipated through the achievement of Communist society. Jean-Francois Lyotard, one of the central theorists of post-modernity, regarded metatheory as central to the definition of modernity, noting that he used the term 'modern'

> to designate any science that legitimates itself with reference to a metadiscourse ... making an explicit appeal to some grand narrative, such as the dialectics of the Spirit, the hermeneutics of meaning, the emancipation of the rational or working subject or the creation of wealth. (Lyotard, 1984: xxiii)

This indicates that Enlightenment theorising right across the ideological board often took the form of metadiscourse. It was also pointed out in the Introduction that Rostow's pro-capitalist theory of stages of growth also fits into this category. Indeed, many development theories, including the neo-liberal vision of development currently endorsed by the IMF and the World Bank, fit into this model. It would also seem that such metadiscourses are linked with foundationalism, a point that is made even more clearly in Lyotard's assertion that:

> Societies which anchor the discourses of truth and justice in the great historical and scientific narratives (recits) can be called modern. (Quoted in Sarup, 1988: 132)

These metadiscourses are foundational. Thus, as we have noted, the SAPs sponsored in the Third World by the IMF and the World Bank find their intellectual basis in the metatheory of neo-liberal economics, which makes a truth claim for itself in identifying itself as a science, the product of reason.

Post-modernity is in large part a reaction against these central elements of modernity, particularly metatheory, foundationalism, and subject–object relations as conceived by Kant, wherein the subject is allocated an over-powerful position in relation to the object. These themes are intertwined in post-modern critiques of modernity, but for the sake of clarity let us deal with the objections to metatheory first.

Lyotard objects to metatheories (what he terms the grand narratives of history) on the grounds that they make universalist claims to truth that tend to exclude and/or repress other interests in society, a critique that has come to be seen as central to post-modernism (hence the numerous references in post-modern literature to discourses that do violence to 'the other'). In his critique of metatheory Lyotard has reference to the Kantian concept of the sublime. This is a complex concept, but for our purposes we can summarize it as denoting phenomena that are beyond our ability to represent them. Lyotard expands on this as follows:

> Nobody has ever *seen* a society. Nobody has ever *seen* a beginning. An end. Nobody has ever *seen* a world. In this case, can we have a sensory intuition of what these questions are about? The answer implied in the critical approach (in Kant's sense) is, no, it's impossible, they are Ideas of Reason (of *Reason*, they're not fantasms). We must consider the Ideas *as* Ideas if we are to avoid illusion: they are like guiding threads ... the same goes for the idea of the proletariat. Nobody has ever seen a proletariat (Marx said this): you can observe working classes, certainly, but they are only part of the observable society. It's impossible to argue that this part of society is the incarnation of the proletariat, because an Idea in general has no presentation, and *that is the question of the sublime*. (In Appignanesi, 1989: 23; the italics are Lyotard's throughout)

In other words ideas such as the proletariat cannot be presented in reality, or in experience as Lyotard puts it. It is impossible to precisely delineate and identify what the concept covers in the real world on Lyotard's reading. It follows that by undertaking such an enterprise and identifying a particular group as 'the incarnation of the proletariat' one is engaging in a misconceived and actually harmful enterprise for a number of reasons. Lyotard hints at one of them in his observations on the positions taken by Burke and Kant on the French Revolution:

> ... I don't share Burke's view of the French Revolution, nevertheless, and I'm guided in this direction by Kant's analysis of the same question, I think he was aware (and Kant certainly was) of the danger of practicing a politics of the sublime. That is to say, to make the terrible mistake of trying to present in political practice an Idea of Reason. To be able to say 'we are the proletariat', or 'we are the incarnation of free humanity', and so on. Kant understood perfectly that that's what happened to the French Revolution. Maybe Burke too was aware of this danger. (p. 24)

This suggests that the identification of a particular group as 'the incarnation of free humanity' was a central factor in the development of a political praxis based on protecting this group by attacking those perceived as the enemy. In short, it led to the 'great terror'. By the same token, it could be argued that the identification of a particular group as the proletariat in the Soviet Union was a factor in leading to the policy of repressing counter-revolutionary elements, one result of which was the Gulag Archipelago.

Lyotard would tend to argue that all metatheories are at least in part addressed to the emancipation of a group such as the proletariat, or the incarnation of free humanity, or the 'Third World' poor, all of which he would identify as Ideas of Reason, which have no presentation in experience. Nevertheless, a praxis is developed based on the identification of such a group and the pursuit of its interests at the expense of other groups. In this sense Lyotard sees all metatheory as being inevitably unjust. It is totalising in the sense that it suggests that its grand narrative is what the whole of history is about, that its truth is the only truth, and that its utopian end-goal for society (whether it be communism, *lebensraum* for the Ayran peoples, or the establishment of mass consumer society throughout the Third World) is the only valid destiny for humankind. One can easily see how commitment to such a metanarrative can lead to an 'ends justifies the means' viewpoint in which terror can seem to be justified in the cause of achieving the perfect society, itself an illusory goal, based as it is on a misapplication of concepts that cannot be realised in practice.

A key to understanding post-modern objections to the modernist formulation of subject–object relations may be provided if we recall Lyotard's reference to grand narratives addressed to the emancipation of the working subject. In such narratives a subject such as the proletariat, or free humanity, is elevated to the position of bearer of world history, which is unfolding with the singular focus of their emancipation. The subject is all-important, or over-determined, whilst the object may take the role of bystander in this process, or that of a resource to be used in the achievement of the destiny of the subject. Apartheid in South Africa might be taken as an example in which the white population, cast as the subject, exploited the other races cast as object, a resource to be used in the achievement and maintenance of 'white civilization'. A slightly different example might see big capital as subject exploiting the natural environment as object. Both of these examples reflect the connotation of an over-powerful subject that maltreats and exploits the object for its own ends. On a more abstract level, the role that Kant allocated to the reasoning subject is that of moulder and shaper of the object. The subject appropriates and renders the object into a form congenial to, or dictated by, the subject. In this view the subject can be seen as imperialist and repressive of others cast in the role of object.

As we have seen, the critique of metatheory is bound up with the issue of foundationalism, given that a central aspect of metatheory is its claim to universal truth. Hitherto we have explained foundationalism as the process of providing grounds for regarding a proposition as the truth, whether those grounds take the form of the logos, of God, or of reason. In order to grasp some of the post-modern objections to foundationalism, we must unpack the contents of this concept a little more. Firstly, it is worth briefly looking at Agnes Heller's definition, which runs as follows:

True statements, arguments, beliefs, and convictions are grounded. If someone asks the question 'why is this so, and not otherwise?' one can have recourse to the grounding of the thing. There are final grounds that cannot be further grounded, but that ground all of the other statements, arguments, and beliefs. If such final grounds are shaken, the arguments, beliefs – truth itself – become ungrounded. Thinking is ungrounded if there is no resting point in grounding. An abyss opens up; one cannot set one's feet firmly anywhere. (1999: 13)

She goes on to examine how to demonstrate grounding:

In a demonstration one has to make recourse to sentences which are for their part nondemonstrable, and which are in no need of demonstration. A principle such as this is a final, ultimate principle, an arche. Without presupposing such principles, demonstrations would go on ad infinitum and nothing could have a grounding. (1999: 13)

An arche is also a point of origin and it is for this reason that many post-modern critics write of philosophers practising 'a metaphysics of origins' (metaphysics is that branch of philosophy that seeks to determine the nature of reality and what actually is real – a fuller definition is given in Chapter 4) when they attempt to ground a proposition. Todd May expounds that:

By 'foundationalism' I mean the project of giving an account (of some object of study) that is exhaustive and indubitable. An exhaustive account is one that says all that needs to be said on the issue. There may be more details to add, but the essence of the matter is captured. An indubitable account is one that cannot be surpassed; it is the final say on the matter. There are, of course, many different ways in which an account may be said to be indubitable. It may be said, for instance, that all other accounts would necessarily run into self-contradiction. This is a strong form of indubitability. Alternatively, it may be said that this account is founded on a bedrock of truisms and with derived inferences so solid that it is inconceivable that a better account could arise. This, I think, is a more standard type of foundationalism, one that we might associate with the work of Descartes or Husserl. (1997: 3)

By founding an account on 'a bedrock of truisms' one is again having reference to an arche. Thus, grounding one's contentions involves identifying an ultimate principle (an originary principle) underlying those contentions and rendering a complete account of the matter at hand.

One of the central objections that post-modern theorists level against foundationalism is that it has been practised in such a way as to marginalise difference. To use May's terminology, the foundationalist tradition 'has allowed itself to function under the illusion that the world and our experience of it can be brought under absolute or indubitable conceptual categories, categories that do not allow for conceptual slippage' (1997: 3). Post-modernists contend that this attempt to define all of reality within the terms of a narrow conceptual framework necessarily leaves out those who do not fit in the framework. As May puts it, 'the scope of different possible lives and identities is often unacceptably narrowed by the pretension of specific conceptual approaches or philosophical viewpoints to give exhaustive accounts of the phenomena in their domain' (1997: 4). In this sense foundationalism is seen to have a totalitarian aspect. It is totalitarian because the categories it grounds tend to marginalise, or eliminate, those who do not fit (as in the case of modernist subject–object relations, it represses the other). Indeed, an explicit linkage can be made with totalitarian regimes, such as that of the Nazis, which attempted in the Holocaust to physically eliminate those who did not fit with its racially defined categories. The same tendencies can be seen to be at work where ethnic cleansing is practised. Consequently, post-modern theorists attempt to avoid foundationalism in the effort to accommodate difference in their theoretical frameworks.

Some support for their position might be garnered from the arguments expounded above to the effect that the modernist faith in reason as a foundation is by no means beyond question. Indeed Dupré argues that one of the central problems of modernity is that philosophers have failed to address the central question that arises with the emergence of the self as a reasoning subject that adjudicates as to what is true knowledge, and that shapes knowledge – the question being: what is the nature of that subject's relation to reality? Dupré suggests that even as modernist analysts have promulgated a culture based on the view that humankind should shape the world in accordance with its needs, even as they have posited the 'meaning-giving subject', they have 'persisted in viewing the real fully established' (Dupré, 1993: 160). They refuse to deal with the question of 'the new function of the subject: How does the subject's constitution of meaning and value affect the very nature of the real?' (Dupré, 1993: 161). Such a viewpoint renders foundationalism at least questionable.

This might lead some to suggest that post-modernism is correct to dispense with foundationalism as a dubious totalitarian enterprise. However, this suggestion brings us back to Heller's point that without grounding, '[a]n abyss opens up; one cannot set one's feet firmly anywhere'. The depth of this abyss may be gauged by reference to Nietzsche, the philosopher whom many regard as the first authentic post-modern voice. Very broadly, his arguments may be summarised as positing that humans are driven by the will to power and knowledge is imbrocated in this drive to acquire power. For Nietzsche it is in fact those who are most powerful who get to define what counts as true knowledge. On this reading reason is no more than a tactic in the struggle between various interests over the question as to which of them should be able to define knowledge. In *Beyond Good and Evil*, Nietzsche made his position of extreme perspectivism clear in a number of statements such as the following:

> Against positivism, which halts at phenomena – 'There are only facts' – I would say: No, facts are precisely what there are not, only interpretations. We cannot establish any fact 'in itself'. (in Pippin, 1991: 95)

Furthermore, he asserted that 'logic is the attempt to understand the actual world by means of a scheme of being posited by ourselves; more correctly, to make it formulable and calculable for us' (in Pippin, 1991: 95). Even science is not spared the corrosive effects of Nietzsche's perspectivism are seen in such statements as:

> It is perhaps dawning on five or six minds that physics, too, is only an interpretation and exegesis of the world (to suit us, if I may say so) and not a world-explanation. (in Pippin, 1991: 95)

From such a standpoint we can be sure of nothing about the world in itself. Indeed, the danger of such a viewpoint is that it can be read as affirming that might is right. Although this is a reductionist reading of Nietzsche, it is a significant one given that it was just such a reading that appealed to the Nazis as legitimising their own crimes. It should be obvious that the danger here is one that Nietzsche himself warned of, that of a destructive nihilism in which values such as truth and falsehood, good and bad, have no meaning, and are ineffective. The problem of dispensing with foundations is that one seems trapped into falling into a relativist abyss.

Some theorists attempt to avoid the abyss by introducing an element of legitimation into a broadly relativist overview. For example, the American neo-pragmatist, Richard Rorty, questions the need for universalistic legitimation, given the existence of various cultural narratives that bind their respective societies together quite effectively (Rorty, in Bernstein, 1985: 164–5). This implies that cultural practices and norms are satisfactorily legitimated by the culture that has produced them. It also implies that criticism across cultural boundaries is illegitimate. Whilst such cultural relativism has the utility of countering imperialistic or racist assertions of the superiority of one culture over another, total acceptance of the principle that all cultures are self-validating means acceptance of various forms of inequality and exploitation and of specific practices such as female genital mutilation, child labour and slavery.

Lyotard takes a similar line, arguing for a politics based on a multiplicity of local discourses, or small narratives (as distinct from the grand narratives that he condemned) that would be legitimised locally, and which would relate to one another on the basis of 'the recognition of the specificity and autonomy of the multiplicity of entangled language games (discourses), the refusal to reduce them; with a rule which nevertheless would be a general rule: let us play ... and let us play in peace' (cited in Wellmer, 1985: 341). It might be suggested that this looks rather like a meta-narrative itself, with its own view of a utopia of small narratives co-existing peacefully on the foundation of a universal morality of non-interference with one another. However, in insisting on the incommensurability of these small narratives, Lyotard encounters the same problem as Rorty, that criticism across narratives would not be legitimate in view of the rule of non-interference. Norris has pointed out that this self-limitation prevented Lyotard from effectively pursuing a critique of the conservative historian, Faurisson, who sought to cast doubt on the occurrence of the Holocaust on the basis that there were no first-hand survivors of the gas chambers to provide experiential proof (see Norris, 1989: 70–85). It would seem then that this version of a narrative-based relativism leaves us no critical weapons with which to critique such movements as Nazism and its allies.

Clearly, modernity has posed a number of problems, most obviously the prevalence of meta-narratives, as well as the overdetermined subject, and foundationalism, all of which mutually reinforce tendencies towards repression and exclusion of the other. A particular problem arises with foundationalism, which in its Kantian formulation provides a somewhat questionable grounding for knowledge, but the absence of which raises the danger of a relativism that effectively deprives us of the ability to make truth claims. We shall now go on to examine how far such issues have manifested themselves in the post-development literature.

2.3   POST-DEVELOPMENT AND ITS DISCONTENTS

A central characteristic of post-development thought is its analysis of development as a form of discourse. Escobar makes it explicit that his analysis is based on the discourse theory of Michel Foucault. As noted in the Introduction, discourse analysis could be seen as promoting the idea that a body of ideas, a discourse, mediates power through its effects on the way we act. As Escobar puts it:

> Foucault's work on the dynamics of discourse and power in the representation of social reality ... has been instrumental in unveiling the mechanisms by which a certain order of discourse produces permissible modes of being and thinking while disqualifying and even making others impossible. (1995: 5)

In other words, discourse and power shape the way that we think and what we see as truth and untruth. Discourse theory sees knowledge as being linked with power in a way that is reminiscent of Nietzsche's identification of knowledge with power. The knowledge that is presented to us through a discourse such as development is not to be seen as a neutral representation or account of reality, but as the product of power relations.

This means that development as a discourse does not originate as an analysis of, and response to, a real world problem of the existence of poor countries that need development. Development is to be seen 'not [as] a natural process of knowledge that gradually uncovered problems and dealt with them', but rather 'as a historical construct that provides a space in which poor countries are known, specified, and intervened upon' (Escobar, 1995: 44–5). This indicates that discourse actually constitutes the problems that it purports to analyse and solve. Thus, poverty considered as a problem of the Southern states, is actually a creation of the development discourse. Having first generated a problem, the discourse then proceeds to construct an analysis of the problem, which then results in the specification and implementation of a solution. The problem analysis and the strategies for its solution all bear the normative imprint of the discourse in question.

Escobar argues that the development discourse emerged from the confluence of a variety of historical factors. Amongst these were a Western concern to win the markets and raw materials of the South for the industrialised North; Malthusian fears about the growth of an impoverished Southern populace; a faith that social problems could be solved by the use of technology; 'representation of the Third World as a child in need of adult (for which read Western) guidance' (Escobar, 1995: 30); and a faith in the efficacy of planning and public intervention in the economy for bringing about change. While all of these factors fed into the genesis of development discourse, Escobar focuses on three central constituents of development theory: first, the need for capital formation and associated factors such as industrialisation, technology and trade; secondly, the need for cultural change and modernization; thirdly, the need to create an institutional base for the analysis of development and for the prosecution of development initiatives. This involved the creation of institutions such as the World Bank, national planning agencies, and development programmes in universities. Escobar emphasises that the development discourse was not in any simple sense the result of any combination of these elements. Rather, it is 'the result of the establishment of a set of relations among these elements, institutions, and practices and of the systematization of these relations to form a whole' (Escobar, 1995: 40). This system of relations may be envisaged as a web of power relationships in which some are empowered, whilst others are disempowered. In the development discourse development experts are empowered through expertise to pronounce on what counts as knowledge and as viable strategies for action. By contrast, the Southern poor are disempowered because they are seen as the problem to be solved by the experts' strategies to make them healthy, literate, or entrepreneurial, depending on what the development experts' objectives are at any particular time.

It is clear that for Escobar, power is central to the operation of development as a discourse. The question is how central? Is his work to be seen as falling into the relativistic trap outlined above? An examination of Escobar's text reveals an oscillation between a number of positions. In the middle of *Encountering Development* he comments that: 'Everything I have said so far in this book suggests that representations are not a reflection of "reality" but constitutive of it' (Escobar, 1995: 130). Thus, Escobar endorses a Nietszchean position in which reality is constituted through the power inherent in discourse. However, in the next sentence he asserts: 'There is no materiality that is not mediated by discourse, as there is no discourse that is unrelated to materialities' (Escobar, 1995: 130). This constitutes a significant modification of the view that discourse is constitutive of materiality, or 'reality'. If materiality is 'mediated' by discourse this is suggestive that it has an independent status from discourse that can be perceived by the observer, in this case Escobar. We can know enough about materiality, 'the world in itself', to know that discourse changes it, or at any rate affects our perception of it.

This gives rise to a contradiction in Escobar's analysis in the following sense. He wishes to contend that the problems and categories that development deals with (such as the urban poor, rural hunger, and so forth) originate with the development discourse itself. However, he seems to be residually aware that this affirmation of the power of discourse to constitute reality entraps him in an ultimately relativist position that discredits his own theoretical commitments. If we can only know reality through discourse, what criteria are available to enable us to make truth claims in favour of one discourse (such as Escobar's post-development position) as compared with another (such as the development discourse)? Rather than directly face this question, and the attendant danger that it leaves him with no arguments for favouring post-development over development, Escobar evades the problem. He lapses into an unacknowledged gesture of implicitly conceding that there is a reality independent of discourse.

Once this concession is made, it follows from this that reality is likely to affect discourse. Indeed, this is acknowledged at various points in *Encountering Development*, as when Escobar refers to development's 'great dynamic quality: its immanent adaptability to changing conditions, which allowed it to survive, indeed to thrive, up to the present' (1995: 44). To be sure, this statement is qualified by an assurance that such changes do not modify the overall system of relations that unify the development discourse. Nevertheless, it is clear that the discourse has to respond to changing conditions, conditions that are beyond its control. This raises the question as to whether or not these responses (or at least some of them) might be examined as genuine attempts to solve real problems, or satisfy genuine needs experienced by the social majorities in the South. Once again, a survey of Escobar's text is suggestive that some of them can. At one point he notes that various forms of poverty have provided lucrative employment for members of the aid 'industry', but: 'This is not to deny that the work of these institutions might have benefited people at times' (Escobar, 1995: 46). In a critique of the Integrated Rural Development Programme in Colombia, he notes:

> One must acknowledge, however, that when the pill is already bitter, running water, health posts, and the like may mean real improvements in people's living conditions. (Escobar, 1995: 145)

Further, whilst Escobar notes the flaws in the Women in Development strategy, he also points out that the UN Decade for Women and WID 'promoted research on women, channeled funds to women's projects, and put First World feminists in touch with Third World women activists, who, in turn, disseminated feminist knowledge among the women's groups with which they worked'. Moreover, the 'fact that international organizations made clear their interest in formulating women's policies at the official level pushed governments in the Third World in this direction' (Escobar, 1995: 184). None of this sits particularly comfortably with the assertion that Escobar makes early in his book, that 'instead of the kingdom of abundance promised by theorists and politicians in the 1950s, the discourse and strategy of development produced its opposite: massive underdevelopment and impoverishment, untold exploitation and oppression' (1995: 4). In the above cases, at least certain groups have attained some benefits from development.

At this stage it should be clear that Escobar's attempted root-and-branch demolition of development is less than fully persuasive. In the attempt to avoid the pitfalls of relativism he is forced to acknowledge that development discourse is at least partially responsive to real needs on the part of the social majorities. If we attempt to locate an explanation as to just why Escobar finds the development discourse so reprehensible, the closest we can come is probably the following passage:

> Development was – and continues to be for the most part – a top-down, ethnocentric, and technocratic approach, which treated people and cultures as abstract concepts, statistical figures to be moved up and down in the charts of progress. Development was conceived not as a cultural process (culture was a residual variable, to disappear with the advance of modernization) but instead as a system of more or less universally applicable technical interventions intended to deliver some 'badly needed' goods to a 'target'

population. It comes as no surprise that development became a force so destructive to Third World cultures, ironically in the name of people's interests. (1995: 44)

As a critique of top-down development this rings true, but it is to leave out of account that a response to the inadequacies of this approach has emerged within the development discourse. What is variously known as 'bottom-up' development, or people's participation, applies a corrective to the over-technical, authoritarian top-down approach by placing an emphasis on local initiative and control of the direction that development should take (this will be examined in greater detail in Chapter 6).

Obviously, the interests that favour top-down development will not necessarily be supportive of initiatives that place control in the hands of the social majorities. Porter has illustrated the ways in which such interests attempt to coopt and appropriate bottom-up ventures and projects (see Crush, 1995: 63–86). However, this does not detract from the fact that there are interests within the development discourse that are attempting to win it for the social majorities. Amongst those interests are many of the social movements that Escobar identifies as the motive force underlying the post-development agenda he subscribes to. One example often cited by Escobar is that of the black communities of Colombia. At a conference of 1993 aimed at the consolidation of a social movement for black communities a set of principles was adopted, amongst which was the following:

Construction of an autonomous perspective of the future. We intend to construct an autonomous vision of economic and social development based on our culture and traditional forms of production and social organization. The dominant society has systematically imposed on us a vision of development that responds to their own interests and worldview. We have the right to give others the vision of our world as we want to construct it. (Alvarez et al., 1998: 203)

Here we have a paradigmatic statement from the grass roots asserting the right of the black communities to shape and control their own development. What is notable here is that this statement is not constructed in terms of a total rejection of development, even though their experience of top-down development has clearly been a negative one. Notwithstanding this negative experience, they are aware that a more positive form of development is available. The key to attaining it is to gain control of the development agenda in order to maximise its benefits, and so this is stated as their objective. An analogous point is made when Escobar notes that the 'fact that women in many parts of the Third World want modernization has to be taken seriously' and that often 'it means something quite different from what it means in the West and has been constructed and reconstructed as part of the development encounter' (Escobar, 1995: 189). Again, this is suggestive that Southern women want control of the development agenda rather than that they want to reject it altogether.

Similar points can be made about the work of Esteva and Prakash. They wax lyrical about the virtues of traditional societies and the efforts of grass-roots movements such as the Zapatistas in seeking autonomy from what Esteva and Prakash variously identify as the global neo-liberal project, modernisation, and development. For example, they paint an idyllic picture of life in the town of San Andres Chicahuaxtla in Oaxaca, Mexico, where the Triqui Indians have taken pains to preserve their culture and traditions. Particular note is taken of the fact that the locally born, but university-trained doctor respects local traditions concerning birth, notably the role of women in assisting one another giving birth. It is observed that whilst he was rarely called, 'nevertheless, he became quite famous in the region for his success in assisting births' (Esteva and Prakash, 1998: 56). One does not need a surfeit of imagination to see how this could be presented as a prime example of community development, finely tuned to local customs, yet ready to supply and input specialist information in contexts where it can be of benefit to the community.

It is also worth noting the unquestioning acceptance of Prakash and Esteva that the university-trained doctor should naturally be male. In lauding the traditional values of Triqui society, they seem to overlook the possibility that such society could also be characterised by customs and values that they might find less desirable, such as sexism (I am indebted to Dr Kate McInturff for this point). This is indicative that they are practising a metaphysics of origin in the sense that they are identifying traditional society as an originating principle or arche, a repository of traditional virtues, from which modern society is a debased breakaway. In order to elevate traditional society to the status of foundational principle, they overlook all of the exclusions that it practises, while emphasising those of modern society, which they consequently dismiss as the inferior of the two.

Throughout their book, Esteva and Prakash tend to base much of their argument on an almost manichaean dichotomy between two ideal types, one depicting the evils of modernity and development, the other celebrating the traditions of the social majorities. This is evident in the following passage illustrating the ill effects of development on the social majorities:

> The damage done to them by state law and education is replicated in every other facet of their lives, including their problems of healing and health. Left without the traditional herbal and other remedies of their communal healers, they must accept the drugs in modern hospitals and related medical services to the masses. (Esteva and Prakash, 1998: 114)

One may have little difficulty in accepting that state law and education cause damage in many cases, but is it credible to claim that the damage caused by development is so universal? In fact, it should be eminently clear that there will be many instances where modern medical facilities will represent the most appropriate, if not the only viable, form of treatment. Modern medicine can inoculate against, or cure, certain ailments that traditional medicine cannot, such as malaria, smallpox, cholera and so forth. This is not to suggest that modern medicine should completely replace traditional forms of healing. Rather, one might hope for the sort of coexistence that was evidenced at San Andres Chicahuaxtla.

Like Escobar, Esteva and Prakash seek to dismiss the concept of development by defining it only by reference to its top-down authoritarian form, directed by intrusive state mechanisms and international aid agencies. They largely ignore the participatory tradition. Consequently, their characterisation of development takes the form of an unconvincing straw man that is easily knocked down. However, if their characterisation is one-dimensional, so is their post-development solution. In his article for Sachs' *Development Dictionary* Esteva argues that those who have been marginalised by top-down development and neo-liberalism have found refuge in what he terms the 'new commons' outside the formal economy. This indicates that these commons overlap substantially with what is often termed the 'parallel economy'. Esteva and Prakash pin their hopes for a post-development emancipatory agenda on the various activities of movements and communities in these commons. Indeed, they provide many examples to illustrate the genius of such groupings in pursuing their own emancipatory projects. Without wishing to cast any doubt on their examples, it nevertheless has to be noted that at no time do Esteva and Prakash show any recognition that marginalisation to the commons, or parallel economy, also means criminal activity, prostitution, low-paid work in dangerous conditions and, if none of the foregoing work, it can mean starvation.

In the Introduction we noted that Prakash and Esteva have difficulty in justifying their endorsement of some groups as emancipatory, while dismissing the claims of others. This is where the problem of relativism manifests itself in their work. Esteva and Prakash openly embrace a cultural relativist position as a cornerstone of their argument against what they see as the depredations of development. They argue that:

> To abstract or to classify with each other, we require common cultural backgrounds. These backgrounds constitute horizons of intelligibility of each culture. (Esteva and Prakash, 1998: 127)

They go on to assert:

> Cultures are incommensurable – a condition which seems clearly uncomfortable for those accustomed to extrapolating their own perception of reality on others. (1998: 128)

Therefore European analytical frameworks, such as development, are inapplicable to Southern societies because they originate within cultural horizons of intelligibility that are incommensurable with those of the South.

However, it is difficult to see how this position can be reconciled with their selectiveness as to which movements and groupings they will allow to be classified as 'post-developmental'. For example, they state that the 'epic' that is 'unfolding at the grass roots' (Esteva and Prakash, 1998: 1) 'does not include all grassroots movements and initiatives' (1998: 3). They go on to specify the Shining Path in Peru, and various groups of Nazis, as being amongst the excluded. In another part of the book it is made clear that Islamic fundamentalism is also discounted (1998: 126). What grounds can they have for discounting these movements, given that at least some of them clearly belong to cultures different from those of the authors, and consequently cultures that the authors should not be imposing their perceptions of reality on? Esteva and Prakash attempt to derive a basis for some sort of cross-cultural understanding as follows:

> Only 'others' can reveal one's own myths; make them visible; eliminate their covers in order to be dis-covered and transcended. But all efforts in that direction will be useless, and the observer will not be able to see or dis-cover unless he or she is ready to love, to listen with care and affection, to identify with what is revealed. None of this entails assimilating oneself to the realities of others; or accepting these without reservations. All it demands is hospitality: the openness to be hospitable to the otherness of the other. (1998: 128)

Having initially argued that one's culture represents the limit of intelligibility, it would now seem that one can gain a special insight into other cultures' myths so long as one proceeds with love, care, and affection. Confusingly enough, Esteva and Prakash preface the above passage with the following comment:

> Each culture is a world, a universe. It cannot be reduced to any other culture's ways of seeing and living reality. It is another reality. (1998: 128)

It seems that Esteva and Prakash are trying to square the circle and failing. They might reasonably argue that each culture is a world to itself with its own system of intelligibility, its own reality, or alternatively they might argue that 'others', or outsiders, can gain a special insight into a culture through a learning process informed by love. What they cannot argue is that both of these mutually contradictory positions are at one and the same time true. Yet that is what they try to do.

Esteva and Prakash fall into a similar relativist trap to that which ensnared Escobar. It will be remembered that Escobar embraced a relativist approach to the effect that power determines knowledge in order to dismiss any truth claims that might be made in the name of development. However, he recoiled from this position when he realised that such a stance left him unable to make any truth claims in favour of his preferred post-development discourse. Similarly,

Esteva and Prakash take a relativist stance to invalidate Northern development interventions in the South, but fall into a morass of analytical confusion when they refuse to accept that it prevents them from making cross-cultural judgements also.

In turning to the work of Majid Rahnema, we shall see that he avoids the trap of post-modern relativism, but his work is characterised by many of the habits of modernist analysis that post-modernism critiques. His analysis resembles those of Escobar, Esteva and Prakash in that good traditional, or 'vernacular', societies, as he terms them, are contrasted with bad development, or modernity. Rahnema begins his critique of development by providing us with a typology of vernacular society drawn from such examples as the Australian aborigines, African hunter-gatherer societies, the Ojibway people of Canada, and the Borana people of East Africa. He differentiates vernacular from modern societies along five axes as follows. Firstly, vernacular societies are characterised by what he terms 'organic consistency', which means that they are bound together by networks of cultural and social relations that form an 'immune system' to protect the community from foreign influences that threaten its integrity. Secondly, vernacular societies are of a limited size. Thirdly, they have simple material and cultural needs, and the modern impetus to accumulate and maximise resources is absent. Fourthly, productive and economic activities are embedded in the culture of such societies rather than being accorded autonomous and paramount significance as they are in modern societies. Finally, the resources essential to the community are defined and produced locally, whereas a modern community's needs can be determined and supplied by advertising and production conglomerates on the other side of the globe.

Rahnema also argues that vernacular societies are characterised by: the propensity to minimise risks to ensure that the community's subsistence is secured; diversification of resources, again to secure subsistence; ecological vigilance based on respect for the sacred role of nature in providing them with the means to live; prudent attitudes to innovation, which mean that change will only be embraced when it is clearly to the whole community's advantage; and a holistic approach to life which means that activities such as hunting are informed by several layers of meaning. Such are the central outlines of Rahnema's model of vernacular society.

He adds the proviso that 'vernacular societies should not be idealized' as they are often characterised by conflicts of interest, deprivations, and they can become violent (Rahnema, 1997: 114). However, Rahnema largely forgets this point as he goes on to describe how development invades vernacular societies like the AIDS virus. The character of this invasion is determined by the fact that it is led by *homo oeconomicus*, a sub-genus of the human species that was born with the emergence of capitalism in Europe. Economic man has few principles other than the free market, the primacy of accumulation and freedom of the individual. Rahnema describes the effect of development on vernacular societies as follows:

> Homo oeconomicus transforms all his prey into 'economic man', like himself, substituting their motives of subsistence and their sense of belonging to the community with those of gain and full individual freedom. (Rahnema, 1997: 119)

By providing schools, making available new products and services, and by casting into doubt traditional beliefs and skills, development validates its own values of individualism, accumulation and the market, whilst undermining the values that maintain the cohesion of vernacular societies.

At this stage it is worth examining Rahnema's characterisations of vernacular society and development a little more closely. In the first instance one might query the status of his model of vernacular society. To the extent that it serves as a model, or a typology, one might reasonably expect that its utility would be as an heuristic device against which traditional societies might be compared. However, Rahnema treats 'vernacular society' as an actually existent category so that he can then base his case against development on its supposed subversion of real vernacular societies. But to what extent do real traditional societies resemble Rahnema's model? A brief examination of the case studies on which he bases his model reveals that many of the vernacular societies concerned exhibit common characteristics that Rahnema seems to have ignored. Most notably, many of the case studies point out that the societies under discussion use a broadly democratic framework for making community decisions (see Norberg-Hodge's case study of 1991 on the Ladakh in India, p. 25 in Rahnema and Bawtree (1997); Clarkson *et al.*'s study of 1992 on the Iroquois in Canada, p. 46 in ibid.; and Dahl and Megerssa's analysis of 1992 on the Boran people in East Africa, p. 56 in ibid.). As will become clear this is a significant omission. However, it is also notable that Rahnema's model evidently assumes that vernacular societies are static. Moreover, it assumes that none of them have, or have had, any propensity towards a process of economic expansion, or what we might term 'endogenous' development. Yet history is full of examples of traditional societies that started from small beginnings to emerge as major trading, and sometimes, military powers. One need only look to the long-established communities of Chinese and South Asians throughout most of Asia to realise that traditional societies in India and China had developed a vigorous dynamic of economic expansion based on trade at quite an early stage in their histories. Certainly, they were significant trading powers before *homo oeconomicus* emerged to corrupt them.

Rahnema might argue that Australian aborigines, African bushmen, and similar hunter-gatherer groups do not seem to have evidenced such expansionist tendencies. However, at no point in his analysis does he stipulate that the category of vernacular society is restricted to such groups. Rather, he tends to apply it generally to indigenous societies in the South. As such it represents an inaccurate characterisation of such societies.

Doubts must also be raised about Rahnema's account of the emergence of development and *homo oeconomicus*. In the first instance, he seems to have confused market capitalism with development. Cowen and Shenton provide persuasive arguments for regarding the emergence of capitalism and development as being related. However, Rahnema seems to think that they are the same thing. This comes as a surprise to those of us who have subscribed to the idea that there could be a socialist form of development. Yet again, we are faced with a post-development critic who has provided a partial definition of development, ignoring those elements of the concept that cannot readily be dismissed by his critique. Yet again, development is set up as a straw man that can easily be knocked down, this time by Rahnema.

As we have already observed, Rahnema's work is reminiscent of those elements of modernity that are criticised by post-modernism, and the partiality of his analysis is central to this perception. It is indicative that Rahnema is developing a post-development meta-narrative based on the foundational concept of vernacular society, or space. The foundational nature of this concept becomes evident when Rahnema uses it to dismiss the role of democracy in the South. Having defined democracy as majority voting, itself an absurdly reductionist position, he asserts:

> Vernacular societies had a much more realistic view of things. Not blinkered by the myth of equality, they believed that the good of the community was better served by those of its numbers it considered to be the wisest, the most virtuous, and hence the most 'authoritative' and experienced persons of the groups – those who commanded everyone's respect and deference. (Rahnema, 1997: 388)

He moves on from this to propound a post-development agenda based on Confucian principles that differentiate society into the masses (the *min*) and 'the good and authoritative people' (the *jen*). The latter would take a leadership role in discussions deciding 'the direction, the quality and content of changes desired by each community' (Rahnema, 1997: 394). To become *jen* one must engage in an individual search for truth and self-knowledge through which one gains the insight to take right actions with regard to others. However, Rahnema concedes that in many traditional societies those in power, supposedly the *jen*, have not lived up to this high standard. Given his dismissal of democracy, it is not clear how Rahnema would propose to prevent unworthy people from gaining power over the post-development enterprise.

Clearly, this is a metanarrative and it is characterised by the exclusory tendencies that post-modern analysts objected to in metatheory. Rahnema has identified a founding principle in vernacular society, which is then defined in such a way as to repress otherness in the shape of the *min*. The latter must submit to the rulership of the *jen* on faith that they will rule justly. At this point it is worth remembering that Rahnema neglected to include any element of democracy in his characterisation of vernacular society, despite the evidence of democratic processes in several of the traditional societies referred to in his source material. Instead, democracy is dismissed in favour of a dialogue led by the *jen*. Rahnema's metanarrative thus proves to be as exclusory as all the others criticised by the post-modernists. His formulation of the foundational principle of vernacular society is exclusory in terms of the data it is based on and in terms of its political exclusion of the *min*.

As mentioned in the Introduction, Cowen and Shenton provide a somewhat more nuanced analysis of development than any of the foregoing commentators. Like Escobar, they approach development as a discourse, tracing its genealogy, or the history of its formation as a concept. Notably, they do not fall into the trap that so many post-development theorists succumb to, that of presenting development as a straw man and then dismissing it. They give consideration to various strands of development thinking, including community development, another development, and even post-development thought in the shape of Marglin and Marglin's reader, *Dominating Knowledge*. Cowen and Shenton argue that all of these schools of thought are derivative of earlier positions that were rehearsed by competing factions in much earlier, chiefly nineteenth-century debates on development.

Their genealogy observes that the classical conception of development tended to be cyclical with periods of growth and decay succeeding one another. In the context of modernity an awareness has grown that growth and decay, creation and destruction, are simultaneous. The idea of progress, the direct ancestor of the concept of development, encompasses both creation and destruction. The old must be destroyed for the new to take its place, as when an old building is demolished in order to make way for a new one. The modern meaning of development grew out of a concern to correct for the destructive effects of progress, such as unemployment, or impoverishment. Thus, development emerges as an intention to manage progress in order to bring about a smoother process of development. One contradiction that arises within this framework is that inducing development necessitates bringing about change, which entails destruction, which is objectionable inasmuch as it implies waste and disruption of the development process itself. This contradiction tends to manifest itself within development theory as an oscillation between two basic positions. At one point modernisers will push for planned and managed development, only to be followed by a reaction against the destruction that such change causes, often couched in terms of an appeal for development to respect traditional cultures and communities. Post-development thinking could be seen as an extreme variant of the latter position, provoked by the intrusive social engineering associated with the Bretton Woods institutions.

Cowen and Shenton's fundamental objection to all these successive schools of development thinking is that they all envisage a process of development 'through the exercise of trusteeship over society'. They define trusteeship as 'the intent which is expressed by one source of agency, to develop the capacities of another' (Cowen and Shenton, 1996: ix–x). Their objection to trusteeship emerges clearly from the following passage:

The jargon of 'authentic' development arises from the way in which development doctrine is stated for people who cannot account for the source of the doctrine itself precisely because they are not developed. Development doctrine becomes jargon when there is both distance and disjunction between the intent to develop and the practice of development; when there is an exercise of power in which the capacity to state the purpose of development is not accompanied by accountability. (Cowen and Shenton, 1996: 454–5)

They maintain that a development theory becomes doctrine when it is advanced and/or adopted as a guide for state policy. Upon acceptance of development doctrine, the state concerned will then take up the role of trustee, guiding the development of a target community, or population. Whilst Cowen and Shenton make it clear that they object to the state's acceptance of this role, they also object to a trusteeship role being taken by other agencies, whether it be the East India Company in colonial India, or NGOs throughout the South. It is not the question of agency as such that is the crux of their objection, but rather the fact that trusteeship entails an act of power over a target population that has no ability to call the agency in question to account.

The fact that an element of trusteeship can be discerned in all of the development strategies examined by Cowen and Shenton raises the question as to whether they have defined trusteeship so widely that development is unable to escape it. In fact they posit a vision of free development based on the work of Sen and Marx. They approvingly quote Sen to the effect that 'the process of development is best seen as an expansion of people's "capabilities"' (in Cowen and Shenton, 1996: 449). Sen indicates what he means by this, quoting Marx's visions of communist society in 'The Critique of the Gotha Programme', where it is 'possible for me to do one thing today and another tomorrow, to hunt in the morning, fish in the afternoon, rear cattle in the evening, criticize after dinner, just as I have in mind, without ever becoming hunter, fisherman, shepherd, or critic' (in Cowen and Shenton, 1996: 449). In this vision humankind has the freedom and capability to 'choose from a potentially infinite set of activities' without ever becoming a wage slave dependent on one source of earnings (Cowen and Shenton, 1996: 449). However, this utopia is premised on the achievement of general material abundance through continual revolutionisation of the means of production, amongst other things. Sen on the other hand is interested in promoting development (i.e. capabilities) in the South, which is usually characterised by a state of relative scarcity. This leads him to argue that the best way of raising human capabilities in such a situation is by raising their 'entitlements'. For most people, their only way of attaining entitlements is by earning payment for labour (e.g. their labour entitles them to a wage that they can use to affect their capabilities). This train of logic leads to the argument that the proper role of the state is to maintain a sound employment policy to raise the number of jobs, thereby positively affecting capabilities. But, as Cowen and Shenton point out, this places the state in a trusteeship role. They also observe that developmental states have often had recourse to such policies, but usually with a view to enhancing production (and thereby the power of the state) rather than out of any concern for people's capabilities. Consequently, this vision of free development also becomes entrapped in the toils of trusteeship.

Indeed, Cowen and Shenton assert that 'it is precisely because development is claimed to be "authentic" that it is nothing more than another kind of trusteeship' (1996: 453). In other words making a truth claim for a development theory is trusteeship. By generating a strategy that we believe will develop the South with the intent to apply it by some means we are engaging in trusteeship. This is suggestive that trusteeship is unavoidable. In the preface to their book, Cowen and Shenton express the hope 'that the idea of development can be recovered from its entrapment in trusteeship' (1996: xv). Unfortunately, their definitions seem to make such an objective impossible.

2.4   CONCLUSIONS

It is clear that in their different ways many of the post-development commentators we have studied fall into the traps we outlined in the first half of the chapter. Escobar, Esteva and Prakash are all bedevilled by various manifestations of a relativism that undermines the truth claims they want to make for their own analyses. Rahnema avoids the latter problem at the cost of formulating his own meta-narrative characterised by its own exclusionary foundationalism. Cowen and Shenton avoid these more obvious traps, but propound a genealogy of development that constructs it as being inescapably trapped in trusteeship.

This leads one to wonder if there can be an acceptable form of trusteeship, bearing in mind that Cowen and Shenton's main objection pertained to a conceptualisation of trusteeship as an act of power by one agency over others, without that agency being constrained by any form of accountability to those others. It also raises the dilemma clearly enunciated by Porter when he reacted to the problem of how to steer a path between exclusivist foundations and nihilism by asking: 'how does one say NO to the totalizing of instrumental reason, yet also say YES to the possibility of justice?' (in Crush, 1995: 86). In the next two chapters we shall examine the work of various critical theorists, particularly Foucault, Habermas, Derrida, and Levinas with a view to examining how far their work can supply answers to these questions.

3 Discourse of Power or Truth?

3.1 INTRODUCTION

In the last chapter we saw that many of the post-development theorists have embraced the concept of discourse in order to critique development. Escobar is probably the most rigorous in his adoption of the concept, demonstrating how discourse theory views knowledge as being inextricably interlinked with power. This key insight is central to their critique of development as a discourse of power, which represses the social majorities of the South. However, if the 'truth' of any discourse is thus compromised by its involvement with power (the fact that power at least in part constituted and shaped that 'truth'), this leaves us very little, if any, ground from which to critique a discourse like development. After all, we would only be offering our own discourse to counter that of the development community, and it would be vulnerable to exactly the same kinds of critique that Escobar and others have made of the development discourse. As we saw, this is exactly the problem that the post-development analysts encountered. They wanted to cast the truth claims of the development discourse into doubt, but still make truth claims for their own discourses. Effectively, they were caught in a trap between endorsing a relativist position that would have enabled them to critique development and taking a foundationalist position that would have enabled them to make truth claims for their various post-development positions. In trying to have both, they tended to lapse into the self-contradiction and confusion that we examined in the last chapter.

Given that the model for the post-development adoption of discourse theory was provided by the work of Michel Foucault, we shall examine his work with a view to determining how he dealt with this problem. As we shall see, it is a problem that he was aware of, and one that he made repeated attempts to solve. We shall also comment on the implications that his work had for issues pertaining to development. Finally, we shall briefly consider a somewhat different approach to such questions by the eminent German philosopher, Jurgen Habermas, who attempted to provide a theory that would enable us to make truth claims, but which would also be inclusive rather than exclusory.

3.2   ARCHEOLOGIES AND GENEALOGIES

Throughout Foucault's work one finds that the relations of knowledge and power constitute one of his core themes, if not *the* core theme. Foucault observed that the rise of the Enlightenment in the eighteenth and nineteenth centuries brought with it a new set of human sciences, such as psychology and criminology. Already existing sciences underwent transformations, for example medicine, which changed from being a matter of classifying diseases to one that was anatomically based. The traditional humanist account of these changes suggests that they were a scientific and humane response to a set of pre-existing problems. Foucault's central thesis was that these sciences constituted discourses through which power was exercised over those classed as criminal, insane, or ill. Whereas humanism examined such discourses as progressive, humanitarian developments – the insane are now given medical treatment rather than being locked away – Foucault argued that the new sciences were a more efficient way of exercising power over target groups such as those classified as insane. Indeed, a crucial aspect of this exercise of power was that these discourses actually created the problematic categories that they were supposed to deal with. Thus, criminology did not emerge in response to the problems associated with the activities of criminals and delinquents, but actually created those categories and began to exercise control over the populace through classifying people into its various categories (it can be seen how Escobar follows this line of thought in arguing that such categories as the 'Third World poor' were created by the development discourse rather than predating it). Central to Foucault's argument was the contention that power and knowledge are inextricably intertwined. In one volume he commented:

> Power and knowledge directly imply one another ... there is no power relation without the correlative constitution of a field of knowledge, nor any knowledge that does not presuppose and constitute at the same time power relations. (Foucault, 1979: 27)

As Simons points out, this relationship is causal in that it is constitutive, 'Foucault's power/knowledge thesis argues that power relations and scientific discourses mutually constitute one another' (1995: 27).

Foucault developed two modes of analysis to examine how power manifested itself in discourse. The first one he termed 'archeology'. This approach aimed at analysing what Foucault called 'the archive', that group of discourses that determined what actually counted as knowledge in a given period. In particular, it focused on discursive practices, which are defined by Flynn in the following terms:

> ... a practice is a preconceptual, anonymous, socially sanctioned body of rules that govern one's manner of perceiving, judging, imagining, and acting. (Flynn in Gutting, 1994: 30)

Foucault argued that practices have two functions, the first 'judicative' in that it establishes rules, norms and determines what will be included and what will be excluded in the discourse. The second is 'veridicative' in that it adjudicates what is to be regarded as true and what is to be dismissed as false. The judicative determines the rules of the discourse, whilst the veridicative legitimates them. This leads Flynn to define the archive as the 'locus of the rules and prior practices forming the conditions of inclusion or exclusion that enable certain practices and prevent others from being accepted as "scientific", or "moral", or whatever other social rubric may be in use at a particular epoch' (1994: 30).

The second analytical tool that Foucault developed was genealogy, which pays more attention to the historical descent of discursive practices. It also focuses more on the imposition of power on the body. As Foucault puts it, genealogy 'poses the problem of power and of the body (of bodies), indeed, its problems begin with the imposition of power upon bodies' (Flynn in Gutting, 1994: 34). Thus, Foucault's genealogical study of penal change, *Discipline and Punish* dealt with the way in which the penal system changed its emphasis from direct punishment of the body through torture, to more subtle methods of control of the body through confinement and the discipline of the prison system. It was in the context of genealogical analysis that Foucault developed his concepts of discipline, subjection and normalisation. The power that is manifest in a discourse 'subjects' the individual in the sense of exerting control over him/her. The prisoner is subject to the control, the discipline of the penal system. Discipline is the method by which people are made subject to the power of discourse. Foucault argued that – 'Discipline makes individuals; it is the specific technique of a power that regards individuals both as objects and as instruments of its exercise' (1979: 170). Discipline is exerted by means of training the individual through the three techniques of 'hierarchical observation, normalizing judgement and ... the examination' (Foucault, 1979: 170). Observation by somebody placed above the individual in a hierarchy ensures that the observer can make a judgement as to whether or not the 'trainee' is performing in accordance with the norms dictated by the discourse. If the trainee falls short of the requisite performance, s/he can be punished until s/he reaches a satisfactory standard. Thus, individuals are trained to act in accordance with the norms of discourse – hence the term 'normalisation'. Examination, as in the context of the academic examination, can test whether or not an individual has reached a required standard of performance as defined by the discourse in question. All of these techniques are ways in which discourse exerts power over the individual, shaping (or normalising) him/her in accordance with the requirements of discourse.

It can readily be seen how such ideas could be applied to development in quite an illuminating manner. If one looks at some of the traditional agricultural development projects that were favoured by the World Bank in the 1970s, one often finds that the central method of reaching the target group, the local farmers, was through what was usually called the Training and Visit Extension method. Extension workers were sent out to the farmers to teach them farming techniques that were usually developed in the West, and that involved the purchase and careful application of costly inputs such as special seeds (e.g. the famous high-yielding varieties associated with the Green Revolution), fertilisers, and so forth. The farmers would be given a loan to cover such costs in the expectation that they could repay it out of their enhanced crop production, which could be sold commercially. At least part of the rationale for such projects was to shift subsistence farmers towards the commercial economy. It could well be argued that such projects were designed to train farmers to perform in accordance with the norms of the capitalist economy, going into debt in order to produce a surplus for (hopefully) profitable sale. Failure by the farmer to perform to expectation (for example by failing to meet a loan instalment) could be disciplined by withholding further loans, or supply of essential inputs. In other words such projects could be seen as exercises in normalisation just as much as (perhaps more than) development.

This is the aspect of Foucault's work that appealed to such post-development analysts as Escobar. However, this is also to leave out of consideration a number of problems pertaining to Foucault's work, and in particular to his account of the close entwinement of power and knowledge. An initial problem arises from the fact that Foucault himself was rather ambiguous in his attitude to his formulation of the power/knowledge relationship. At certain points it is clear that he wanted to condemn the entwinement of power with knowledge, as in *Madness and Civilization* when he asserted that 'the world that thought to measure and justify madness through psychology must justify itself before madness' (Foucault, 1965: 289). Similarly, he wrote in *Discipline and Punish* about the spread of discipline through society to the effect that 'insidious leniencies, unavowable petty cruelties, small acts of cunning, calculated methods, techniques, "sciences" ... permit the fabrication of the disciplinary individual' (1979: 308). All of this indicates that the power/knowledge relationship has negative and repressive effects, the effects that Foucault associated with the subjectification and normalisation of people. However, a perusal of *Discipline and Punish* reveals the statement that: 'Power produces; it produces reality, it produces domains of objects and rituals of truth' (1979: 194). Foucault even averred that: 'Discipline "makes" individuals' (170). On the one hand it would seem that the power of discourse is repressive, insidious, and cruel, and that it should be called to account for the way that it classifies and treats the 'mad'. On the other hand, power is what produces our reality and ourselves as individuals. The power/knowledge combination is ambiguous in being both repressive and productive at the same time.

This recognition of the ambivalent nature of power was manifest in Foucault's own political involvements. For example, Rabinow points out that in 1983 Foucault was interviewed by an official representing one of France's largest trade unions on the difficulties facing the social security system. Rabinow notes that, although Foucault had recently been writing on the genealogy of the welfare state, he did not raise such issues as discipline and normalisation, and the 'interview contained a clear and unequivocal commitment to the positive value of social security' (Rabinow in Gutting, 1994: 209). His comments illustrate the ambiguous nature of power, noting that French welfare legislation had been effective at relieving certain problems, such as those of housing shortage and an inadequate medical system, but at the cost of the development of a rigid bureaucracy and syndrome of growing dependence on welfare. One might have expected that Foucault would condemn welfare statism as yet another instance of normalising power. Instead he points out that withdrawal of welfare services would result in the marginalisation of large numbers of people who need housing, medical and other types of assistance. His attitude towards the welfare state is probably best summarised in his statement during the interview that 'the objective of an optimal social coverage joined to a maximum of independence is clear enough' (Rabinow in Gutting, 1994: 209). In other words, Foucault's ideal objective would have been to minimise the normalising tendencies of the welfare state whilst maximising its benefits for its clients.

It is not difficult to see how this line of thought could be adapted to deal with the question of aid and development for the South. Certainly, the activities of the World Bank and various other aid institutions are normalising and generative of relations of dependency. However, the practical commitments of Foucault should have told his post-developmental followers that reform of development might be a better strategic option than their decision to dismiss the development discourse root and branch. It is particularly notable that Foucault completely dismissed the notion of withdrawal of welfare services on the grounds of the deprivation that such a measure would cause. As we have seen, Escobar and the other post-development commentators are well aware that levels of deprivation are increasing in many parts of the South, including areas that are already subsisting at a lower level than that of Foucault's France. In the face of such circumstances it seems almost inexplicable that they could be so dismissive of the possibilities of reform.

A partial explanation may be suggested in terms of the post-developmentalist's rather simplistic reading of Foucault, a reading that does not encompass the ambiguity of the power/knowledge relationship. They have eagerly embraced the insights into the repressive aspects of subjection and normalisation, but have completely ignored the recognition that these same processes can also be productive and beneficial. This failure is all the more lamentable given that many of the Southern groups whose interests the post-developmentalists seek to represent (e.g. the new social movements) are able to see that what they need is not the end of development, but the reform of development (for example the black communities of Colombia cited in Chapter 2).

Even more doubt can be cast on post-developmental use of Foucaultian theory to reject development. The reason for this is that the above-mentioned ambiguity about the power/knowledge relationship finds its origins in a fundamental problem at the heart of Foucault's formulation of this concept. This problem manifests itself as 'performative contradiction'. If all discourse is produced by relations of power, then why should we regard Foucault's theories as anything more than just another discourse? Foucault presumably presented his theories to a public audience because he regarded them as valid and wished to make validity claims for them. Yet, his theories put all validity claims into doubt by arguing that acceptance of a theory is determined by power relations rather than by that theory's accuracy or truth. His act of making a validity claim was in contradiction with the content of his theory (hence the term, performative contradiction). In short, according to Foucault's own logic there is no reason to accord any more credence to his theories than to any others. This suggests that his work falls into the relativistic trap identified in Chapter 2, where what we regard as knowledge is determined by power, the implication being that we cannot establish what actually is true about the world in itself.

This not only casts doubt on the validity of Foucault's theories but also implies the absence of any normative basis for resistance to power. Charles Taylor argues that Foucault's logic leads to the following conclusion:

> There can be no such thing as a truth independent of its regime, unless it be that of another. So that liberation in the name of 'truth' could only be the substitution of another system of power for this one. (Rouse, in Gutting, 1994: 104)

It may be that the present power system, or regime is repressive, but there is no reason to suggest that any regime that might replace it will be better since its truth is merely the determination of its power. Nancy Fraser adds to this the observation that:

> What Foucault needs and needs desperately are normative criteria for distinguishing acceptable from unacceptable forms of power. (1981: 286)

In the absence of some means, such as a foundation, for determining what is true and what is not, we have no grounds for resisting oppression, or for determining which forces or movements are genuinely emancipatory and which are not. White argues that Foucault leaves us unable to make distinctions between such movements as the Ku Klux Klan and the women's movement (1986: 430). Clearly, this represents a severe problem for the post-development observers. In the first instance, they would have no basis for claiming that their post-development regime would be any less oppressive than development, and secondly, they would be unable to distinguish between grass-roots movements, identifying some as emancipatory and others as not.

Many of Foucault's advocates attempt to muster a defence of this relativism along the lines that his approach opens up and maximises strategies of resistance rather than focusing on one strategy and closing all others off, this being the mistake made by traditional emancipatory strategies. For example, Rouse argues as follows:

> The question Foucault's critics insistently raise is, Why engage in *these* struggles rather than others? Why take *this* side rather than an opposing one? Their concern is that without some legitimating standpoint to provide reasons for them, these choices will always be arbitrary or dictated from 'without'. But Foucault was perfectly prepared to offer reasons for his choices of struggles and sides. He was equally prepared to offer reasons and evidence for the statements he made.
>
> What Foucault was not prepared to do was to see these choices, statements, and reasons as more than a situated response to a particular political and epistemic configuration. (Rouse, in Gutting, 1994: 112)

In other words, Foucault would explain his choice of strategies on a case-by-case basis in order to avoid claiming some sort of independent authority, or general applicability for his views. Foucault explained himself in the following terms:

> My point is not that everything is bad, but that everything is dangerous, which is not exactly the same as bad. If everything is dangerous, then we always have something to do. So my position leads not to apathy, but to a hyper- and pessimistic activism. I think that the ethico-political choice we have to make every day is to determine which is the main danger. (Quoted by Rouse, in Gutting, 1994: 112)

In short, different situations require different responses and the decision (the ethico-political choice) that has to be made is how to respond to each particular danger. Rouse comments on this that 'such a choice requires a considered and informed judgement, but cannot be further legitimated by any appeal to a science or a principle of right' (1994: 112). One wonders just what the decision-maker in question will consider and what will s/he inform him/herself of. In deciding to support one strategy, or course of action, over another, it is impossible to avoid reference to such issues as which one is most likely to achieve such aims as justice, equity, a satisfactory balance between social solidarity and openness to the other. Consideration of such issues inevitably involves reference to some principle of right. Furthermore, what will the decision-maker inform him/herself of if not the facts of the situation in some attempt to discern a true account of the problem at hand. A relativist stance leaves us unable to judge which course is the most just, or to establish the facts of the case, even on a day-to-day basis.

Another option would be to take a cultural relativist position and argue that Foucault's theory is meant to be applied by the analyst to his/her own culture. However, as we saw in Chapter 2, such an approach makes cross-cultural criticism impossible. It would mean that the post-development school would have no means of examining new social movements in cultures other than their own, either to critique or support them – and, as we have seen, they want to do this. Furthermore, a culturally bounded methodology seems singularly inappropriate to a globalising world where different cultures are coming more and more into contact. Cultural relativism offers no solution to the problems posed by Foucaultian analysis for post-development thinking.

Simons tries to defend Foucault's relativism by arguing that his critics rely on concepts such as truth, value, future and subject as regulative principles to critique power, whilst such judgements conceal and involve other acts of power. He notes that such principles as justice are identified as neutral and therefore suitable for use in judging whether an action is right or wrong. However, such principles are not neutral. One's understanding of justice is mediated through discourse and is consequently determined by power. Thus, the principles that we try to use for guidance in making a decision, or for criticising power, are themselves products of power. Simons goes on to ask whether such principles are really necessary in order to judge whether or not we need to resist ethnic cleansing. He argues that the compromised nature of regulative principles leads to cynicism, and those who are disappointed by bias in philosophy become 'nihilists unable to differentiate between good and bad regimes, between just and unjust policies, or between tyranny and freedom' (Simons, 1995: 67). The irony here is that Simons himself has reference to regulative principles such as truth and value in the above sentence. How else can he judge between good and bad, justice and injustice, other than by reference to such principles as truth and value. Even the judgement that some people become nihilists and that this is undesirable is predicated on such principles. One might also question Simons' apparent assumption that the imbrocation of these principles with power renders them illegitimate. It is worth remembering Foucault's ambivalence towards the power/knowledge formula, sometimes criticising the repressiveness of power, but also regarding it as productive of knowledge. This suggests that the involvement of principles with power does not necessarily render them invalid.

Indeed, Habermas argues that Foucault was a crypto-normativist in that he regularly made indirect reference to norms such as justice and equity in his regular critiques of the asymmetries of power. Norris makes a similar point in examining Foucault's later work, arguing that it displays

> a tension that results on the one hand from Foucault's espousal of a Nietzschean or private-estheticist creed (e.g. relativist), and on the other from his growing recognition that the truth-values of enlightened thought ... cannot be abandoned without at the same time renouncing any claim to promote or articulate the interests of justice, autonomy, and human emancipation. (Norris, in Gutting, 1994: 184)

Support for the point of view that Foucault was trying to resolve the problems arising from relativism can be drawn from Visker's analysis of the development of Foucault's theorisation of the relationship between knowledge and power.

Visker argues that Foucault was trying to reconcile the following aspects of his relation of power/knowledge. First, the role of power in producing all knowledge means that power is a positive force. Secondly, if knowledge is acted on, or modified by power, this suggests that the validity claims of knowledge are compromised. Thirdly, power is active in discourses to invalidate competing discourses, and to set the rules for what should be excluded as false. If the first point is indicative of a positive role for power in the constitution of knowledge, the latter two points are suggestive of a negative role in which power distorts, or represses knowledge. Foucault wanted to maintain the idea that power produces knowledge, but also be able to condemn the repressive aspects of power. In addition he wanted to criticise the humanist account of the origins of discourses, which sees them as responses to pre-existing problems. As we saw, Foucault contended that a central aspect of the power of discourse is the way in which it generates a set of categories into which it classifies people. Thus he rejected the claims of psychiatry to be a scientific response to the problem of how to deal with mental illness, arguing instead that it generates its categories of mental disturbance and then exercises power over people by classifying them into those categories. Foucault regarded the humanist account of discourse as being characterised by a metaphysics of origins, which essentially means that it attempts to legitimise discourse (to provide a foundation for it) by explaining its origins in terms of science and humanitarianism, rather than power. Such are the various strands of argument that Foucault sought to reconcile in his account of discourse.

Visker suggests that Foucault's initial formulation of the power/knowledge relation was presented in *Histoire de la Folie*, in which he argued that the discourse of power represented in psychology and psychiatry distorts madness. In this instance Foucault was enabled to criticise the power of discourse to distort knowledge, but the implication of this viewpoint is that there is an originary madness that predates the discourse under analysis. The danger in this is that Foucault was coming close to replicating a humanistic metaphysics of origins inasmuch as he conceded that there is a preceding problem that psychiatry addresses. This is in violation of his thesis that discourse actually creates the categories and problems that it addresses as a part of its imposition of power. As we saw in our discussion of Escobar, once pre-existence of a problem is conceded, it becomes possible to accumulate evidence and arguments to suggest that humanism may be correct and that the discourse under analysis might be a legitimate response to the problem that it treats (Escobar's concession that development dealt with actual existing problems led to an accumulation of evidence that contradicted his thesis that development was completely destructive in its effects). A critique of power that concedes the existence of the problem that power claims to address undercuts itself to the extent that it legitimises intervention by power. In sum, this formulation of the power/knowledge relation enabled Foucault to criticise power, but not as radically as he would have wished. Ironically, the assertion that psychiatry distorts 'madness' also undercuts the productive role of power in constituting knowledge. This formulation of power/knowledge combines the worst of both worlds from a Foucaultian point of view. It practises a metaphysics of origins, thus detracting from the critique of power, but also critiques power in such a way as to undercut any view of power as productive.

Foucault attempted to solve the above problems by changing the formula under consideration to power-truth. He defined truth as 'the ensemble of rules according to which the true and the false are separated and specific effects of power attached to the true' (Visker, 1995: 112). In the context of this formulation power is not identified as creating new objects of knowledge. Rather, the truth is seen as exercising power because its nature is to introduce a set of rules of exclusion on which to judge what is true and what should be dismissed as false. Selection and exclusion create orders of truth, that is to say, discourses. The problem with this account is that it gives us no basis for criticising individual discourses, or for comparing the validity of different discourses. Once a set of principles has been established as determinant of the truth for a particular discourse they cannot be questioned from within that discourse – they are simply the truth! However, we have no basis for questioning those principles from outside the discourse. Different orders of truth, or discourse, are constituted by means of contingent exclusions and selections. This means that the difference between these orders of truth is contingent. We cannot point to one as being more valid than the others. In sum this formulation also falls into the relativistic trap.

Foucault next turned to genealogy to solve his problems. He attempted to remove the danger of a metaphysics of origins by emphasising the role of discipline and normalisation in imposing the order stipulated within particular discourses. This put an emphasis on the contention that discourse is constitutive of the knowledge that it disseminates. Even so, this still did not eliminate the problems of metaphysics of origin on the one hand and relativism on the other. When Foucault wished to criticise the effects of discipline on the body – that is, its imposition of order on the body – this inevitably implied an intact originary body that was being violated. In other words, it invoked a metaphysics of origins in which the truth of an originary body was being distorted by power. On the other hand, an insistence that all knowledge was produced within discourse simply reproduced the situation whereby each discourse, or truth regime, validated itself internally, whilst leaving no external standpoint from which the validity of different discourses could be compared. Thus, relativism reared its ugly head yet again.

A pattern is emerging from this analysis. We can see that when Foucault wanted to criticise the effects of power in discourse, he inevitably found himself making an appeal to some form of metaphysics of origins in order to demonstrate how a discourse had adversely affected some category of phenomenon that pre-existed it. The originary category might be madness that had been distorted by the normalising effects of psychiatry, or the originary body itself, which had been violated by the imposition of some discipline. Whatever the particular case in point might be, the effect was always to imply that discourse addressed some pre-existing reality, which contradicted Foucault's dictum that discourse generated all of its own categories. By contrast, whenever Foucault insisted on the principle that power constitutes all knowledge, he found that he had no vantage point from which to criticise discourse, consequently falling prey to relativism.

Visker identifies one final attempt Foucault made to escape this dilemma. Foucault pointed out that Nietzsche held that every identity is an equating of the unequal. Each individual's identity is a product of power. It has been formed through disciplinary techniques and normalisation. In this way Foucault tried to identify a space for criticising power at the individual level. However, he quickly fell into a familiar trap, arguing that individuality is a product of power that must be resisted. As Visker puts it, this 'critique of individualization, of discipline (etc), seems to be borne along by a kind of nostalgia for an anonymity which must have preceded individualization' (1995: 123). Again, Foucault lapses into an appeal to an originary state. In addition this view replicates the disadvantage of some of his earlier positions in being uniformly negative in its attitude to power.

At this stage Visker proposes his own effort to render Foucaultian analysis consistent so that it is able to criticise the effects of power manifest through discourses. He suggests that critique be focused on those discourses that systematically misrecognize their origins in the sense that they conceal their exclusionary practices to legitimate themselves. This means that exclusions and discipline are not condemned in themselves. Instead discourses that misrepresent themselves, claiming that they are not exclusive or coercive in any way, would become the target of critique. However, Visker undermines this position by pointing out that discourses may have to misrecognize their origins to legitimate themselves. Upon initial consideration it may seem quite likely that this is the case. After all, how can a discipline make validity claims if it acknowledges that its definition of the truth is selective in the sense of being exclusionary? Such a viewpoint might lead us to dismiss Visker's suggestion on the grounds that all discourses are bound to misrepresent themselves in this way. However, this would be a premature conclusion, because Visker's amendment of Foucault moves in the direction of a position advanced by Jacques Derrida, whose work we shall examine in the next chapter. We shall leave Visker's point for now, but it will be worth remembering when we examine Derrida's thought.

What does seem clear is that Foucault himself was never able to resolve the problems involved in wishing to claim that all knowledge is constituted by power, but then also wishing to make validity claims and criticisms himself. In the final analysis he does fall into the trap of performative contradiction, questioning the validity claims of all discourse without taking sufficient account of the status of his own critique as discourse. Foucault is unable to avoid the relativist trap.

A number of commentators have argued that one way to escape the dangers of relativism would be through recourse to a system of ethics, although it would have to be one that does not take the form of a foundational system of rules, which would make its own exclusions. Foucault actually developed an ethical outlook that was strongly bound up with his view of how the individual might resist disciplinary and normalising power. At the core of this viewpoint are what Foucault termed technologies of the self, which the individual can use to create and empower him/herself. One strategy of self-creation/empowerment involves transgression of social norms such as those involving sexuality, drug use, and so on. It has to be pointed out that all of these strategies are very individuated and do not really tell us much about how Southern social movements might set about improving their conditions of life, or how Northern interests might help them. Smart reaches the conclusion that although Foucault's ethical care of the self and technologies of the self might have something to offer at the individual level, it is clear that they are aimed at self-liberation as opposed to concern for the other. Smart contrasts Foucault's care of the self with the ethics of Emmanuel Levinas, which is based on the idea of an infinite responsibility for the other, suggesting that modern mind-sets over-emphasise care for the self at the cost of care for the other (Smart in Moss, 1998: 89–90). It can be seen how Levinasian care for the other might have more relevance to development issues than Foucaultian care for the self, and we shall be examining Levinas' ethics in the next chapter.

Foucaultian discourse analysis is clearly a powerful tool, and certainly one that strongly influenced many post-development analysts. As we have seen, the application of concepts like normalisation can tell us much about the operation and effects of hierarchies in development projects for example. However, discourse theory carries with it severe problems pertaining to its relativistic nature. Whilst one might accept that there is an inevitable entwinement of knowledge and power, the complete identification of knowledge with power in Foucault's discourse theory means that one has no basis for critique. Certainly, existing discourses are expressions of power, but so is any conceivable critique. And if all discourses are equally effects of power, there is no reason to prefer one to another. This line of thinking leads to a political quietism that cannot be afforded by anybody who cares about those whose living standards (whose lives!) are being endangered in the South. Foucault himself recognised this inherent danger of relativism and tried to overcome it in his own work. His failure to do so, a failure by one of the most eminent of modern thinkers, should make us cautious of the nostrums of post-modernism. In view of this we shall move on to a brief analysis of the theories of Jurgen Habermas, also an eminent philosopher, but an uncompromising critic of post-modernism.

3.3 DISCOURSE ETHICS AND THE PROBLEMS OF APPLICATION

Habermas is concerned with many of the problems that concern post-modernism, notably the tendency for foundationalism and the over-determined subject to result in exclusions. However, Habermas tried to solve such problems by taking a radically different path from that of the post-modernists who usually ended up embracing relativism in one form or another. Instead he has developed a discourse ethics, an ethical theory of communication. A good point at which to start our exploration of discourse ethics is by noting with Habermas that discourse is not simply the product of the individual subject's reflections, but is a communicative event involving a number of debaters. It is an inter-subjective phenomenon. On this basis he argues that it is possible to identify rules of discourse to enable ethically acceptable decisions to be made, which all concerned parties agree upon. Furthermore, the outcome of discourse can be foundational in the sense that it is based upon the agreement of all involved parties as to its truth, or validity.

Hohengarten provides an admirably brief and clear account of the basis of Habermasian communication theory, which I shall quote at length:

> Habermas argues that linguistic meaning is constituted communicatively. The smallest unit of communication is the utterance put forth by a speaker *together with* the 'yes' or 'no' taken toward that utterance by a hearer. Every utterance contains a (stated or implied) prepositional component *p* that predicates something of an object. However, even in the case of an assertion, the meaning of the utterance is not determined by *p* alone. The full meaning of an utterance depends equally upon *how* this propositional content is being put forth – whether it is being asserted, commanded, confessed, promised, etc. This *force* of the utterance is given by its *illocutionary component*, which may be made explicit by a performative clause: 'I assert …,' 'I command …,' 'I confess …,' 'I promise…,' and so on. But every utterance in fact makes three distinct *validity claims*, only one of which is thematized by the illocutionary component. That is, with her utterance a speaker makes a *truth* claim relating to the objective world of states of affairs, a *rightness* claim relating to the social world of normatively regulated interpersonal relations, and a *truthfulness* or *sincerity* claim relating to the world of experiences to which the speaker has privileged access. Each of these validity claims is universal in two senses. First, each of them is raised, either implicitly or explicitly, in every speech act; they are *universal formal features* of linguistic communication. But secondly, each also lays claim to *universal validity* for what it claims to be true, right, or truthful. That is, the validity that is claimed cannot be restricted to 'validity for the speaker', or 'validity for this specific group'. Validity means validity for every subject capable of speech or action. With any utterance, then, a speaker lays claim to three dimensions of validity that *transcend* the particular context or the

linguistic community in which the utterance is made. (Habermas, 1992: viii–ix)

Thus, we cannot avoid making validity claims whenever we speak, because they are the condition of communication. Habermas moves from this to suggest that 'the speaker can illocutionarily influence the hearer and vice versa, because speech-act typical commitments are connected with cognitively testable validity claims' (Held, 1980: 337). In other words, validity claims are linked to an implicit, or explicit obligation to justify, or prove the claim. If there is doubt about the validity of a claim it can become a subject of discourse.

Held adds the insight that: 'Behind all smoothly functioning communication is a background consensus based on the mutual recognition by all interlocutors of validity claims. It is assumed that all participating subjects could, if the background consensus is brought into disrepute, justify their views and attitudes' (Held, 1980: 339). A number of values are implicit in this vision, such as, for example, the ability and freedom of all participants to fully and truthfully state their cases. In fact, this ideal situation seldom, if ever, actually pertains. Most of the institutions in which discourse takes place are characterised by some form of hierarchy, which limits free expression of views or grievances (even if informally) by those on the lower rungs of the ladder. However, Habermas argues that we have to proceed as if there is free and full communication in order to maintain the smooth functioning of society, polity, and all the other institutions that rely on communication. He moves on from this to work out the conditions required to reach such a state, which he terms an ideal speech situation (ISS). His object in this is two-fold, firstly to provide a model for political and other forums of discourse, and secondly to provide a comparison against which existing forums and discourses could be measured.

In the first instance, Habermas sets the condition for an ethical discourse in terms of universalisation. He defines his principle, (U) as follows:

(U) For a norm to be valid, the consequences and side effects of its general observance for the satisfaction of each person's particular interests must be acceptable for all. (1990: 197)

This principle means that the interests of all participants must be observed, or taken into account in any discourse. In this way

Habermas tries to prevent any emergence of the exclusionary tendencies that post-modernists find so objectionable in foundationalism. In order for (U) to be validly observed, it must be put into implementation via a process of discourse, rather than being entrusted to an individual. This consideration leads to principle (D), which is defined thus:

> (D) Only those norms can claim to be valid that meet (or could meet) with the approval of all affected in their capacity as participants in a practical discourse. (Habermas, 1990: 66)

Blaug points out that by specifying a practical discourse, Habermas is stipulating a strong preference for actual discussion of the norms so that a genuine consensus can be reached by all participants rather than being imposed by sectional interests. There are two further sets of conditions that are necessary for (D) to be achieved, the first set taking the form of what Blaug calls 'symmetry conditions'. These pertain to practical discourses, and state firstly:

> that each participant must have an equal chance to initiate and to continue communication; second, [that] each must have an equal chance to make assertions, recommendations, and explanations, and to challenge justifications. (Benhabib, 1986 quoted in Blaug, 1999: 11)

These conditions ensure symmetry in the sense that everybody has an equal chance to speak and put their views. They are complemented by what Blaug terms a 'reciprocity condition', which stipulates that relations between participants must take the following form:

> All must have equal chances as actors to express their wishes, feelings, and intentions; and ... speakers must act as if in contexts of action there is an equal distribution of chances 'to order and resist orders, to promise and refuse, to be accountable for one's conduct and to demand accountability from others'. (Benhabib quoted in Blaug, 1999: 11)

These symmetry and reciprocity conditions are designed to ensure that principle (D) is achieved and that all those affected by a norm are enabled to discuss it in discourse. This, in turn, ensures that (U) is achieved and only those norms are adopted that are the result of a genuine consensus of all those involved in discourse. The central points in this model are that discussion should be free, all sides should have an equal opportunity to air their views, and the resultant outcome should be universally acceptable. Such are the delineations of what Habermas terms the ideal speech situation. In the sense that it provides us with a method for producing universally acceptable norms, or outcomes, this model of discourse represents a method for producing foundational information.

It can be seen that this model of the ideal speech situation provides a number of improvements over many of the political and bureaucratic institutions that take fundamental decisions about our lives. Obvious central points are that it is inclusive and open, which certainly differs from the secretive, hierarchical, and exclusive working ethos of agencies such as the World Bank, the IMF, and so on. Of course, Habermas is well aware that it is unlikely that such agencies will ever voluntarily dispense with their bureaucratic barricades. Nevertheless, he offers the model as a reference point. To be sure, it is one that may never be obtained in all its transparency, but if one could move agencies such as the IMF towards a greater measure of openness, it would constitute a substantial improvement on the status quo. However, two central criticisms have been aimed at the model. The first pertains to the crucial issue of implementation and implies that the model is too abstract to be of use in concrete situations. The second suggests that Habermas tends to assume a telos of consensus, with the consequence that he under-emphasises difference. Both of these problems are potentially serious for any planned use of discourse ethics in a development situation.

Firstly, we shall deal with the question of implementation, focusing particularly on Blaug's account of Habermasian discourse theory, since he is one of a few commentators who have dealt extensively with its practical implications. Blaug argues that it is almost impossible to empirically establish how close a model is (whether it be conceptual or actual) to the requisites of the ideal speech situation. He points out that Kemp breaks down the components of unfettered discourse into four components, or axes. These entail imperatives against exclusion, against silencing, against disempowerment, and against intimidation. If all these transgressions of free speech can be eliminated from a model one can reasonably say that it is representative of an ideal speech situation. Our problems begin with the realisation that this situation is most unlikely to pertain in reality. This means that some sort of compromise will have to be accepted. We may have to accept a low standard of performance along one axis in order to gain higher standards along two of the other axes. For example, a model may be more inclusive, but still allow silencing and intimidation of the less powerful. We face even more complex problems if we are contemplating change from one model to another, or modification of an existing model of discourse. It is eminently possible that one model will offer gains along one or two axes, but will compare poorly to alternative models along the other two axes. Indeed, this is likely to be the case with any model under consideration. They are all likely to have variant shortcomings along one or more of the four axes. How then are we to decide which model is best? One way to solve the problem would be to assign weights to the axes so that, for example, high inclusiveness would weigh heavier than silencing. A model that was inclusive but silenced some contributors would then be more acceptable than a model where inclusiveness was low, but everybody present was allowed to speak. The example shows how pointless such an arrangement would be. Freedom of speech is not served by assigning greater importance to inclusiveness if those who are included are silenced. It is pointless to assign weights to each axis as all of them are equally necessary to the ideal speech situation. Dryzek has pointed out that if one compares the Third Reich to American democracy, one gets a clear result, with the USA winning along all four axes. Blaug argues that this is so obvious 'that it hardly constitutes a use of theory at all' (1999: 49). It is worth noting that such comparisons are somewhat more relevant in parts of the South where violations of fundamental democratic rights are commonplace. However, this does not detract from Blaug's basic point that it is almost impossible to determine how close a model of discourse is to the ideal speech situation, except in the most obvious cases.

Habermas tries to ameliorate these problems of judgement by stipulating that the model of the ideal speech situation does not enable us to design the institutions in which discourse takes place. Clearly, it points in the direction of democracy, but the nature of the institutional arrangements should itself come out of discourse by those likely to be affected by such arrangements. The reason for this is that the model gives us a procedure for reaching valid decisions, but does not itself represent a decision about the ideal arrangement of discoursive institutions. There are numerous possible institutional configurations that could at least go some way towards meeting the conditions of the ideal speech situation. Consequently, rather than agonising over which one best meets those conditions, the choice between them should be left to those involved.

This stipulation is part of a distinction Habermas makes between establishing the validity of a norm through discourse and deciding whether or not it is appropriate to apply the norm in particular circumstances. Habermas maintains that a norm could be valid, but inappropriate to a specific situation. This is indicative that discourse can be seen as having two stages, or moments. Again, this can be seen as an attempt to clarify problems relating to judgement by dividing the process into two parts involving two different types of judgement. The first moment involves justification of a norm, which concerns questions of rightness and validity. If the norm passes this test it is available for application. This prompts the second moment of discourse, which concerns choice of courses of action in a particular situation, and which Blaug consequently refers to as a discourse of application. This moment of discourse moves away from the question of validity and focuses much more on questions such as how a particular course of action is likely to work in the situation under analysis. Such considerations would involve side-effects, as well as impact on particular groups with different needs. Blaug characterises this stage of discourse as follows:

> Judgement, here in regard to the right course of action in a specific situation, involves the appropriate application of a norm. Discourses of application are therefore, in effect, discourses of judgement. (Blaug, 1999: 88)

This leads to a further set of problems relating to judgement, and in particular, the way in which the principle of universalisation is supposed to be reflected in both the moments of discourse. With regard to the first moment, that of identifying universal norms, Blaug argues that 'the principle is so strong a presupposition that it has the effect of leveling a whole series of differences that exist between concrete individuals and groups, not least among them, that of gender' (1999: 91). Different individuals and groups have different social backgrounds, which imply different opportunities and needs. To treat them exactly alike by applying the same norm across the board can be inappropriate and unfair in such circumstances. Such a practice would be exclusory.

As to the second moment, that of judgement, or application, critics have questioned whether it would be possible for participants to actually reach a decision in the conditions identified by Habermas. Blaug characterises such criticisms as 'falling under the rubric of a threatened "cognitive overload" of participants' in discourse. He continues:

> According to the principle (U), we are called upon to evaluate and reach agreement on the consequences and side-effects of a universal adherence to a norm for each individual concerned. The question is, how could such an evaluation ever be possible, particularly when we confront conflicting norms and the need to justify exceptions. (Blaug: 1999: 92)

In other words it would seem to be impossible to achieve a decision in the face of such demands. Habermas tries to solve this problem by arguing that universality is supposed to apply to the first moment of discourse, which deals with identification and testing of universal norms. It is not meant to be applied as a principle of application.

This raises the question of what guidance the participants in a discourse have to ensure that their decisions pertaining to applications are morally acceptable. As Blaug points out, 'just because a majority of the German electorate voted for Hitler in 1933 does not make their choice morally right' (1999: 93). It is clear from this that, to be moral, a judgement of application must have reference to some sort of principle of right, but such a conclusion returns us to the problem of just how we relate a particular context bound problem, or decision, to a universal norm, or principle of right.

Blaug suggests a potential solution in abandoning the principle (U), which would mean that we give up trying to produce universally applicable norms in discourse. This would mean that the outcome of discourse would no longer be grounded in the sense of being universally agreed on. However, this leaves principle (D) untouched. It will be remembered that (D) sets the conditions for achieving an inclusive, egalitarian and open discourse. To the extent that these are universal rules for the conduct of a morally valid process of discourse, they still provide a foundation for discourse in the sense of ensuring that the process through which decisions and norms are produced is a fair and impartial one.

Unfortunately, this takes us back to the problem of how we are to judge whether or not an actual discourse fulfills the criteria for (D).

We have already seen how Kemp identifies four axes of unfettered discourse, against exclusion, against silencing, against disempowerment, and against intimidation. We also saw how difficult it was to establish how far a particular instance of discourse fell short of, or satisfied the various criteria. This line of argument seems to have taken us full circle, leaving us no nearer to solving the problem of how to apply Habermasian discourse theory than we were before.

Blaug argues that this problem can be finally solved with reference to Wittgenstein's approach to 'the problem of universals'. Rather than attempting to enumerate all the various ways in which a particular example of discourse replicates, or departs from the ideal speech situation, the Wittgensteinian approach suggests that one should search for family resemblances between the Habermasian model and the example under analysis. Wittgenstein elucidates this approach by arguing that if one wishes to examine games one should proceed as follows:

> Don't say 'there must be something common, or they would not be called "games"' – but look and see whether there is anything common to all. – For if you look at them you will not see something that is common to all, but similarities, relationships, and a whole series of them at that. (Quoted in Blaug, 1999: 109)

Having examined a number of games and identified a number of similarities and differences, he goes on to argue:

> We see a complicated network of similarities overlapping and criss-crossing: sometimes overall similarities, sometimes similarities of detail. I can think of no better expression to characterize these similarities than 'family resemblances' … And I shall say: 'games' form a family. (Quoted in Blaug, 1999: 109)

Blaug moves on from this basis to argue that it is more practical to examine discourses in this way rather than by trying to ascertain how closely they resemble the ideal. He suggests that 'instances of communication that are distorted bear family resemblances to each other, and nothing short of our individual and collective exposure to a great array of instances of distortion will allow us to make such judgements' (Blaug, 1999: 109–110). Blaug cites Dreyfus and Dreyfus to the effect that: 'it seems that beginners make judgements using strict rules and features, but that with talent and with a great deal of involved experience the beginner develops into an expert who sees intuitively what to do without applying rules' (1999: 111). Thus, practice will enable us to recognise distortions as they recur from one case of discourse to another. This cuts short the laborious task of enumerating all the ways in which a discourse diverges from, or coheres with the ideal, and suggests that judgement is related to a well-honed intuition that has gained in sensitivity through practice.

None of this is to contradict the model of the ideal speech situation. In order to be free and fair, discourse needs to meet the conditions of the model, such as the dictates against silencing, intimidation and so forth. However, Blaug argues that in order to judge whether or not a discourse is free and fair, one does not need to investigate such detail. Rather, a practised eye can make such a judgement on the basis of family resemblances.

It might be argued that the reliance on expertise counselled here opens the process of discourse up to abuse. Experts in a position of influence may use their situational power to dilute freedom of discourse to their own advantage. Blaug guards against this eventuality by introducing his own Principle of Preservation (P) into the model. He defines this as follows:

(P) Outcomes of, arrangements for, and intervention in political judgement, must not, if they are to be normatively valid, have the effect of damaging the general capacity to make political judgements. (1999: 125)

He clarifies that what constitutes damage must be decided in discourse by all participants, though noting that such developments as exclusionary practices and the creation of an underclass would obviously violate (P).

If such argumentation goes some of the way to alleviating doubts about the practicality of implementing Habermasian discourse theory, we still have to contend with the critique that its consensual assumptions tend to efface difference. We have already seen that a part of the motivation for discarding principle (U) was that universalisation tended to efface difference. However, it can be argued that the tendency to assume consensus still remains despite the sacrifice of (U). In support of this contention we shall quote Warren to the following effect:

To the extent that we deal cognitively with the relations that situate us in the world, we do so through the medium of language. But since language is not private, since it is learned and sustained intersubjectively, we are also motivated to come to understandings with others about the validity of our claims about these relations. Habermas's important proposition is that cognitive veracity depends on intersubjective validity.

Thus, in Habermas's view we are always motivated towards consensus in speech (about facts, norms, aesthetic judgements, and the like) simply because validity claims in language are pragmatically embodied in the relations to the world through which we reproduce ourselves. (Warren, in White, 1995: 180)

In short, the nature of language itself motivates us towards consensus. Critics point out that there are other factors involved in our socialisation, not least culture – and, of course, cultures can be significantly different along a number of axes.

Warnke has tried to develop a theory that accommodates cultural difference into Habermasian discourse theory. She uses the work of Taylor and Walzer, particularly referring to the example of Quebec in Canada, to demonstrate that the demands of cultural difference can justifiably modify the condition of discourse that all be treated with absolute equality. In Quebec the status of the French language is guaranteed through such regulations as those stipulating that commercial signs have to be written in French, and that businesses with over 50 employees must be run in French. There are no such protections for the English language in Anglophone Canada. Consequently, such measures run against the principle of equal treatment. Warnke argues that such examples of differential treatment can be justified where the survival of a culture is at stake. That culture will be of value to those who have been brought up within it. Moreover, one's culture shapes the way in which one understands the principles of discourse and the question of what makes a discourse just. This means that cultural difference must be taken into account in the principles of discourse if those who are different are not to be marginalised and unjustly treated. Where there is a cultural minority, this fact can justify differential treatment for that minority to protect their culture, and to ensure that they have a voice in discourse rather than being drowned out by the majority view. Warnke concludes on this basis that 'if forms of life have to be molded to meet liberal principles halfway, as

Habermas stresses, we need to emphasize the opposite as well: that the meaning of consensually justified principles must be molded to meet cultural values and traditions half-way as well' (Warnke, in White, 1995: 136).

This line of thought opens up a controversial issue which Warnke aptly formulates as the question, 'are all judgements about what makes a good life of equal standing here? Must principles be modified to accommodate the integrity of any culture?' (Warnke, in White, 1995: 136). The question being addressed here is that of multiculturalism, which is often associated with a relativist point of view that all cultures are to be regarded as equal. Sometimes, the claims associated with this position take the form of the higher nonsense associated with 'political correctness', a doctrine that is notable for its failure to offer any explanation why it is correct. Warnke uses Taylor's arguments to demonstrate that it is possible to respect other cultures without any sacrifice of analytical rigour. Taylor suggests that we start from the presumption that any culture that has been embraced by a society for any substantial period must have something to offer to all mankind. However, there is no automatic confirmation of this presumption. It must be confirmed, or disproved by the study of that culture. In other words, this is not a relativist position that automatically assigns equal status to all cultures.

Nevertheless, the operating assumption in approaching a different culture must be that it has worthwhile insights that must be respected. Such respect dictates that we do not force our own values on a foreign culture, precisely because such a culture may have new insights to offer about those values. Warnke cites Gadamer to the effect that we should assume that other cultures have insights to offer so that we can learn about them, but also so that we can review our own values and prejudices in the light of what we have learned. Taylor and Walzer suggest that we can guard against the possibility of according legitimacy to totalitarian, or repressive, cultures by adherence to a principle of tolerance. This would stipulate that, while it is legitimate to adjust the principles of discourse to encourage preservation of cultures (for example by fostering their languages, history and customs), no culture can be allowed to try and eradicate others. Warnke points out that a principle of tolerance could be legitimated through discourse organised along the lines specified by Habermas.

At this stage it is worth reviewing Habermasian discourse theory with a view to examining whether or not it does provide a foundation for ethical discourse, whilst being open to the other, and providing a model that is capable of implementation. It is clear that the original formulation of the ideal speech situation by Habermas raises problems of implementation. The salient question is whether the modifications proposed by Blaug solve those problems. There is some merit to the proposal that experienced participants in discourse will be able to recognise whether or not the conditions for free discourse have been met on the basis of family resemblances. One question is whether or not this might advantage experienced negotiators, thus creating a situation of inequality on the basis of expertise (albeit informal expertise). Blaug's principle (P) provides a safeguard against this in stipulating that nothing must impair the general capacity to make decisions. However, he also notes that the requirement for efficient decision-making procedures is likely to lead to trade-offs against the deliberative practices that are central to an effective discourse. In order to counter this tendency he suggests that any trade-offs must be generally agreed and evaluated in discourse. Blaug further points out that provision of full information is necessary to ensure an informed and useful discourse and so maintenance and monitoring of quality of information are essential to preserve the effectiveness of discourse. His final suggestion for maintaining the vitality of discourse is to ensure that meetings and consultation remain regular. As we have seen it is practice that hones discourse skills and ensures that participants have the abilities required to recognise a valid discourse. One sign of the decline of discourse is when meetings become less frequent and a group of activists become influential in the sense of beginning to take decisions for others. It is clear from all this that there are no measures that can guarantee the continued validity of a discourse even in Blaug's modified terms – only precautions against its decline, which are dependent on the continued motivation of the participants.

A further level of complexity is added by the need to make provision for difference, a factor that is somewhat undervalued in the original model of the ideal speech situation. Warnke emphasises a valid point in showing that it may be necessary to accord differential treatment to different groups so that minority interests can be protected and preserved. She applies this at the level of relationships between different cultural groups, arguing for a principle of tolerance, through which the values of each culture will be respected, but not to the extent of allowing one culture to harm other cultures. This makes it clear that a group that wished to practise ethnic cleansing would be unacceptable. The principle works effectively with a relatively simple example, such as that of one group that wishes to repress another. A very salient question would be how far the principle provides us with a tool for distinguishing between competing claims made by different minorities, or underprivileged groups. For example, certain schools of feminism argue strongly in terms of positive discrimination for women. Various less privileged cultural groups in the world allocate a role to women that many such feminists would see as discriminatory. Clearly, there is a conflict of interests here between such cultural groups and feminists. Which out-group is to be most respected under the principle of tolerance? The answer is unclear, because feminists could argue that women are being damaged by their position of cultural inferiority, whilst representatives of that culture could argue that any change in gender relations would fundamentally damage their cultural traditions. This is, of course, a debate that is very much alive in development studies, and it is one that even Warnke's revision of the Habermasian model of discourse seems unable to answer. The principle of tolerance seems to be rather a blunt instrument in that it does not give us much help in deciding how to weigh the merits of different (and often competing) claims for tolerance.

Clearly, the problems of actualising the ideal speech situation, and in such a way as to recognise difference, are severe. The strong probability is that they cannot be overcome. But if we are to compare the theories of Habermas and Foucault with a view to assessing which one has the most to offer the South in terms of providing a model for progress, there can surely be very little doubt that Habermasian discourse theory is far more directly useful. None of this is to deny Foucault's intellectual achievement, but his critique is hampered by problems of relativism, and he provides nothing that can even approximate to an emancipatory strategy at the collective level. By contrast, Habermas provides a model for an egalitarian, emancipatory discourse. We have seen that maintenance of a truly egalitarian discourse is likely to be problematic, and that there are problems relating to the recognition of difference in discourse. Nevertheless, Habermas gives us concrete guidelines as to the conditions for free discourse. Blaug has even represented them as a checklist (see Table 3.1). It can be seen that by following this checklist, an organisation could attempt to design and maintain an equal process of discourse. Certainly, it should be obvious to most observers of development issues that development bureaucracies at all levels would at the very

Table 3.1: Conditions for Egalitarian Discourse

Stage of Decision Process	Perceptual Issues	Procedural Issues
1. Problem Recognition	Identifying need for decision, that maintains participation.	Do all have the right to raise problems and set the agenda?
2. Deliberation	Gathering relevant data. Recognising fair deliberation and choosing procedures that maximise deliberation.	Can all join in debate? Is debate arranged fairly? Is damage to deliberative capacities minimised?
3. Decision	Recognising when to close discussion and how best to make decision.	Method for making fair, efficient decision that minimises threat to participation.
4. Implementation	Seeing how and when to implement.	Procedures for implementation and handling problems.
5. Evaluation	Assessing fairness of process and damage to participation.	Procedures for evaluation and re-assessing participatory damage.

Adapted from Blaug, Ricardo, *Democracy: Real and Ideal*. (Albany: State University of New York Press, 1999), p. 142.

least be made more responsive to the interests of local cultures and those who live at the grass roots, if their mandate involved addressing such issues as whether everybody could join in the debate, whether the debate was fair, and so forth.

In conclusion we can suggest that the formalism of the Habermas approach (that is to say, the fact that it can be represented as a model to be followed by different organisations, communities, and other groups involved in discourse) is both a strength and a weakness in terms of our purposes as developmentalists. It is a strength in the terms just mentioned – that is to say, it provides a model that can be used in development discourse to try and ensure that development is emancipatory. Its weakness is that implied by the term 'formalism', in that discourse can become a mere formality, an observance of set rules that departs from the spirit of equality that the rules were designed to guarantee. Once rules are set in stone they can quickly become instruments of oppression and exclusion, even if they were once designed to achieve the opposite. This could only exacerbate any tendencies in Habermasian discourse theory to efface difference and that is an eventuality that cannot be afforded in the sphere of development. It is for this reason that the next chapter will examine a body of theory that develops an ethics based on the recognition of difference.

4 Towards a Development of Least Violence?

4.1 INTRODUCTION

This chapter will survey the work of Jacques Derrida on deconstruction, together with a briefer analysis of the writings of Emmanuel Levinas on ethics. Derrida is the better known of these philosophers (although the work of Levinas has received greater attention in recent years, partly as a result of Derrida's interest in, and respect for Levinas' original work on what some have dubbed a post-modern approach to ethics). However, Derrida's reputation is somewhat mixed, indeed, one might say that he is notorious amongst some of the more establishmentarian stalwarts of the Anglo-Saxon school of philosophy. Such figures are wont to assert that Derrida advocates precisely the sort of relativistic and nihilistic standpoint that we have identified as the central risk of much post-modern thought, and by extension of post-development thought. One might wonder why it is worth giving consideration to Derrida's work, given that the last chapter argued that Foucault's thought provided a problematic basis for post-development analysis precisely because he never succeeded in ridding his own work of relativistic tendencies – this being despite plentiful evidence to the effect that he was aware of them, and wished to counter the implications that they had for undermining his own discourse. If we are to dismiss Foucault for his failure to dispel relativism, why would we go on to embrace a philosopher who explicitly advocates a relativist position and polemicises against reason?

In fact, any slightly more than cursory examination of Derrida's work reveals that his deconstructive thought is by no means relativistic. Moreover, he has repeatedly denied that he is post-modernist, or that he is against reason, or the Enlightenment. Nor is he against metatheory, as his recent engagements with Marxist thought have shown (although he does share Lyotard's suspicion of their tendency to make absolute validity claims). This chapter will argue that Derrida's work is far preferable to the post-modernity embraced by post-development analysts in that it provides us with a much better way of dealing with the dilemma that has been a central theme in this book, that of how to avoid the totalising and exclusory tendencies of foundationalism, whilst not falling into the trap of relativism. Furthermore, a deconstructive approach informed to some degree (the extent being a matter for debate) by Levinasian ethics, provides a much more effective basis for future development thinking and activity than any of the post-modern alternatives hitherto examined.

The debate on Derrida's thought, its implications (if any) for politics, and its relation to ethics (particularly the ethics of Levinas), has unfolded over a period in excess of 30 years. In order to render this very complex work accessible, we shall focus on those elements of it that are relevant to our own immediate concerns with development. Whilst this means that we will examine deconstruction in general, it also means that we shall only be paying cursory, if any attention to aspects of Derrida's work on such issues as phenomenology, psychoanalysis, literary theory and so forth (this being work that is influential and important in its own right, but of limited relevance to the concerns of this book).

The complexity of Derrida's writing has also meant that the full implications of his thought have only been appreciated in philosophical debate quite gradually. It would probably be fair to say that many observers initially grasped how the deconstructive technique destabilised foundationalism, but without fully understanding how it avoided a relativist stance. It was only gradually that it became clear that Derrida did not fall into a relativist trap, a development signalled by the emergence of such commentators as Bennington, Beardsworth, and Hobson. Similarly, the synergies and parallels between Derrida's thought and that of Levinas were most notably pointed out by Simon Critchley in his influential study, *The Ethics of Deconstruction* – only for other critics, including Derrida himself, to react by noting that there were substantial differences between Derrida and Levinas as well as similarities. In order to unpack the respective insights into Derrida's work made in each successive phase of debate in an understandable way, we shall examine them in order of their emergence in that debate. Thus, we shall firstly examine what I characterised as the initial understanding of deconstruction and how it destabilises foundationalism. We shall then move on to assess the political relevance of this initial 'model' of deconstruction with brief reference to a relatively early attempt to effect a reconciliation with Marxist theory. Alan Ryan undertook this ambitious project before Derrida had himself written any substantial commentary on Marxist thought, but in retrospect it can be seen to bring out some interesting associations between deconstruction and Marxism. Having made an initial examination of the technique of deconstruction and its political implications, we can proceed to focus on Critchley's synthesis of deconstruction with Levinasian ethics in order to examine the possibilities for a deconstructive ethical politics. This will be followed by a fuller consideration of deconstruction to indicate how it provides an analytical method that avoids 'totalisation' as Derrida terms it (this means that deconstruction does not practise the exclusionary closures that characterise foundationalism), but that does not lapse into the relativistic nihilism that is often associated with post-modern thought. Our explication of this point will enable us to conduct a fuller re-examination of the political and ethical implications of deconstruction. The chapter will conclude by addressing the issue of deconstruction's relevance to development by examining some of Derrida's own observations on modern international politics that were undertaken in 'a spirit of Marxism' in his volume *Specters of Marx*.

4.2   DECONSTRUCTION AT FIRST SIGHT

Deconstruction is often described as being fundamentally a critique of the two intimately related branches of philosophy known as 'metaphysics' and 'ontology'. *The Concise Routledge Encyclopedia of Philosophy* defines metaphysics as involving 'two types of inquiry', the first involving 'the most general investigation possible into the nature of reality' with a view to determining whether or not 'there are principles applying to everything that is real'. The second type of inquiry 'seeks to uncover what is ultimately real'. The entry goes on to note that:

> Understood in terms of these two questions, metaphysics is very closely related to ontology, which is usually taken to involve both 'what is existence (being)?' and 'what (fundamentally distinct) types of things exist?' (2000: 567)

If we move on to *The Oxford Companion to Philosophy* we find a particularly useful entry on ontology from our point of view because it focuses on precisely the feature of ontology and metaphysics that deconstruction seems specifically to attack. The entry reads as follows:

> Ontology, understood as a branch of metaphysics, is the science of being in general, embracing such issues as the nature of existence and the categorial structure of reality. That existing things belong to different categories is an idea traceable at least back to Aristotle. Different systems of ontology propose alternative categorial schemes. A categorial scheme typically exhibits a hierarchical structure, with being, or entity as the topmost category, embracing everything that exists ... (in Honderich, 1995: 634).

The entry continues, but the central point for us to note is that ontology and metaphysics attempt to explain reality by means of classifying things into categories and hierarchies. It can be seen that such an enterprise is totalising in that it attempts to explain reality comprehensively, producing an exhaustive and indubitable account to recall the terms that Todd May used to describe foundationalism. Indeed, foundationalism can be seen as an intrinsic part of the ontological enterprise inasmuch as ontology entails examining reality in terms of categorial schemes, in which concepts are organised into a hierarchy, some of which will be fundamental (constituting grounding, or foundational principles), whilst others come lower in the hierarchy, often defined as being in some way derivative from the foundational concepts. It can be seen then that, as with our examination of foundationalism in Chapter 2, this process results in the marginalisation of certain categories, whilst others are privileged, and this is certainly one of the tendencies in ontology that Derrida critiques through deconstruction.

This becomes evident in the following explanation of deconstruction provided by Christopher Norris:

> Deconstruction locates certain crucial oppositions or binary structures of meaning and value that constitute the discourse of 'Western metaphysics'. (Norris, 1989: 71)

In each pairing one concept is preferred to the other, which is seen as derivative from the primary concept. Thus, philosophers have traditionally tended to locate an opposition between speech and writing in which the former is preferred to the latter since it connotes presence and direct communication, whereas writing implies absence and a consequent potential for meaning to be lost and distorted. Derrida's contention is that such closure is artificial. For the grounding principles to stand as foundational concepts they must be self-sufficient and self-identical. Derrida asserts that all concepts are referential, being produced by what he terms 'differance'. This is a conflation of the words 'differ' and 'defer'. Derrida's contention is that the identity of every concept is established inasmuch as it differs from or defers something else. Ryan demonstrates this with the following example:

> The word 'for' takes on a meaning and function only in a language chain that relates it differentially to other words from which it differs in use, function and place in the chain, and which it defers, in the sense that such other words as 'of' are implied by 'for', but their onset is delayed or put in reserve if 'for' occupies the focus. (Ryan, 1982: 12)

Each element derives its identity by reference to another element. This implies that the pairing of concepts, in which one is viewed as a foundation and the other as derivative, cannot be validated. The relationship between the concepts is one of mutual dependence and is irreducible in the sense that neither concept can be isolated and regarded as self-sufficient. Derrida terms this 'radical alterity'.

This line of thought leads to a view of deconstruction as consisting of displacing the dominant concept in such binary pairs by demonstrating that the subordinate concept has an equal claim to be considered as a condition of possibility for the system of ideas under analysis. Displacement is achieved by finding what Derrida refers to as an undecidable element in the theory linking both the foundational and the subordinate concept in such a way as to subvert the validity of claims which privilege the former concept over the latter. Thus, to return to our initial example of the philosophical preference for speech over writing, it can be noted that speech is a signifier in the same way that writing is. As such it can also be subject to slippage in meaning and this is the element of undecidability that displaces speech as a foundational concept.

It might be asked what bearing this understanding of deconstruction has on politics, or on development? Ryan provides us with the beginning of an answer in his analysis of the implications of deconstruction's polysemy and referentiality for political praxis. He points out that the left has traditionally attempted to organise itself monolithically, with a view to fighting for the oppressed in a bipolar struggle between capital and labour. Such a process of organisation runs the all-too-familiar risk of centralisation and authoritarianism.

Deconstructive analysis is suggestive of a more complex terrain in which a multiplicity of diverse struggles take place between whites and blacks, landlords and peasants, men and women, autocrats and civil societies, capital and labour constituting only one of these axes of conflict. He notes that: 'Materiality is plural and differentiated; it separates and multiplies, rather than forming identities that have a permanence akin to that of ideal forms which bear authority.' Ryan concludes from this that it is possible for various leftist forces to pursue simultaneously their different yet articulated struggles (Ryan, 1982: 216–18). Similarly, it may be concluded that the so-called 'Third World' is irreducibly diverse and that the old monolithic views of development must give way to a plurality of different projects. The variant social forces and political interests of the South must be allowed to develop their own various conceptions of what is to represent development. This suggests a position identical to that of the post-development theorists, that is, one of support for the new social movements. It might also be taken as implying that the proper role for Northern interests, such as development agencies and non-governmental organisations, must be to support and assist these indigenously rooted forces in their diverse projects of empowerment and progress (although I shall argue in favour of a rather more proactive approach below).

Unfortunately, this line of thought leaves many of our fundamental questions unanswered. Not least, it fails to provide an answer to the related questions as to which of the social movements should be deemed worthy of support, or should support be given to all Southern movements that identify themselves as developmental? The latter option is clearly unacceptable given that the post-development analysts seek to exclude certain movements from their emancipatory agendas, such as Sendero Luminoso. Indeed, one can sympathise with the wish to deny aid and comfort to movements that may be corrupt, or that wish to promote the aims of one group at the expense of another, or others. However, as we have seen, the post-developmental embrace of a post-modernism that endorses a relativist position denies them the analytical tools to distinguish between movements in terms of what makes them acceptable or unacceptable. As we argued in the introduction to this book, an ethical approach is necessary to make such distinctions. It may also be asked if this deconstructive view of development implies that Northern agencies may only properly take a reactive role in Southern development, only responding to existent Southern initiatives, or can they take a more proactive role, making their own initiatives? If the answer to the latter question is positive, this raises the issue of what form such initiatives might take given the need that development should be rooted in local demands and perceived needs. This also implies that an ethical dimension is necessary to our consideration of these issues inasmuch as Northern agencies will need guidelines of some description to guide their interventions, and such guidelines will inevitably involve an ethical component to indicate what may or may not be morally acceptable.

The problem with such a proposal is that most ethical systems are characterised by the drawbacks that the term 'system' implies. They tend to become hard-and-fast sets of rules that are supposed to apply universally, and at all times. In other words, they exhibit all the problems that Derrida associates with ontology, becoming rigid, total systems that set up universal categories of what is good and what is bad. As such, they are unable to respond effectively to change, or to viewpoints derived from different moral systems, which are liable to be dismissed as merely wrong, or actively evil. In this sense they marginalise and exclude. For Derrida this is one of the abiding problems of ontology, that it propounds intellectual systems that make claims to total coverage of all issues relevant to the system under analysis, and consequently claims universal validity, while in reality it actually represses and excludes those factors, or categories, that do not fit neatly into the system. This is what Derrida often refers to as 'ontological totalisation' (although he also uses such terms as 'ontologisation', or simply 'totalisation', to refer to essentially the same phenomenon). Most ethical systems can be seen as thoroughly ontological in terms of their totalising and exclusory tendencies. As such, they are clearly unsuitable for our purposes in that we require an ethics that can accommodate and, indeed, welcome the multiple differences of the South. According to some analysts, such a system is propounded by Emmanuel Levinas. Moreover, according to some observers, notably Critchley, it is complementary with Derridian ideas of deconstruction. We shall move on to an examination of these claims in the next section.

4.3   ETHICS AS FIRST PHILOSOPHY

Levinasian ethics does not take the form of a code of moral rules that claims to be universally valid. Instead Levinas locates the ethical impulse in the individual's proximity to the other, or to 'the face' of the other. The individual's primary realisation that there is an other prompts the ethical response to take unlimited responsibility for the other. This radical response to be for (as opposed to being with) the other is not prompted by any request, order, or activity from the other, but is simply a response to the existence of the other, or to the other's face.

This view of ethics is quite different to traditional philosophies of ethics, which are founded in ontology. Levinas explains the difference in the following way. The ontological tradition locates our ability to acquire knowledge in our self-aware, intentional activity of reasoning through which we 'grasp' the unknown in the real world, render it comprehensible to ourselves, and thus reaffirm our own being in (and control of) the world. This is a self-centred account of being in which I explain my existence by appropriating the other of the unknown, or the non-identical, and rendering it identical (comprehensible). As Hand puts it:

> Intentionality reduces wisdom to a notion of increasing self-consciousness, in which anything that is non-identical is absorbed by the identical. In this way, self-consciousness affirms itself as absolute being. (Hand, 1989: 75)

Levinas points out that this is traditionally thought of as a pleasurable activity of reflection and understanding and he consequently terms it '*bon conscience*'. Thus, ontology examines being in terms of intentional reasoning.

However, Levinas notes that prior to this intentional reasoning, there is a non-intentional awareness that is passive. All of us are aware that there is an I that simply exists before and as we address our capacity for intentional reasoning to issues in the world. Because of its passivity and 'being-without-having-chosen-to-be', this pre-reflective form of consciousness cannot affirm itself through a process of appropriating knowledge. As Levinas puts it:

> ... it is not guilty, but accused; and responsible for its very presence. It has not yet been invested with any attributes or justified in any way. (Levinas in Hand (ed.), 1989: 81)

Therefore, it is an unhappy form of consciousness that is unable to explain itself, which prompts Levinas to call it '*mauvaise conscience*'. In the face of its inability to explain or affirm itself, this *mauvaise conscience* faces the problem of justifying its existence. This problem is solved by the encounter with the other, which prompts the *mauvaise conscience* to justify its being by entering a relationship of proximity with the other in which it commits itself to an unlimited responsibility for the other. Such is the origin of ethics for Levinas. The ethical moment is that of taking responsibility for the other.

It will be noted that this form of ethics is not grounded in ontology, which treats of intentional consciousness. Instead, it originates in pre-reflective consciousness. Therefore, the first question in philosophy is not that of why we exist (the classical question of ontology), but rather that of how we justify our existence. Ethics is a first philosophy and is prior to ontology.

Bauman examines the implications of this as follows:

> Morality has no 'ground', no 'foundation' (again, two uncompromisingly ontological notions, untranslatable into the language of morality, having no referents in the moral world 'before' ontology, in the 'otherwise than being'). It is born and dies in the act of transcendence, in the self-elevation over 'realities of being' and 'facts of the case', in its not-being-bound by either. (Bauman, 1993: 73)

A little further on Bauman elaborates further:

> The awesome truth about morality is that it is not inevitable, not determined in any sense, which would be considered valid from the ontological perspective; it does not have 'foundations' in the sense that perspective would recognize. (1993: 75)

There are no reasons in the ontological world of calculations and rational actor models to explain or enforce morality on us and it is clear that the extreme demands of the moral impulse can be refused. Morality can only be achieved through transcendence over ontology. As Levinas puts it:

> There is a utopian moment in what I say; it is the recognition of something which cannot be realised but which, ultimately, guides all moral action ... There is no moral life without utopianism – utopianism in this exact sense that saintliness is goodness. (Wright *et al.*, 1988: 178)

This is not the sort of utopianism that metatheories engage in, where we are enjoined to achieve the institution of a totalising utopia in real life (e.g. communism, the untrammelled free market, etc.). In fact an essential aspect of morality is the awareness that one cannot achieve saintliness, that it is impossible to do enough to fulfil one's moral responsibilities, but nevertheless the willingness to make the attempt in any case.

The question arises as to what might prompt people actually to be moral given that the demands of Levinasian morality are so extreme. In the first instance it is worth repeating that the ethical impulse can be refused. However, Levinas does provide reasons as to why it might be accepted (in addition to the discomfort of the *mauvaise conscience*). His central proposition is that our relation with the other forms our self-identity in large measure. Whereas for Sartre the self or the ego is born by discovery of and resistance against the implicit threat of the other, Levinas argues that the self may be born through union with the other. This is due to the unique and individual responsibility one accepts in entering the relation of proximity with the other. Such responsibility cannot be transferred to anybody else. It is uniquely one's own and it is what makes us unique individuals who cannot be interchanged.

Critchley also draws on Derrida's commentary on Heidegger in *Of Spirit* to argue that language is a product of responsibility to the other. He argues that any question is 'always already pledged to respond to a prior grant of language' (Critchley, 1992: 194). The question has a prior responsibility to answer this pledge, which has not been chosen by the questioner. Where then does language originate? Critchley answers as follows:

> The origin of language is responsibility ... My language begins as a response to the Other. In short, it is ethical. (1992: 195)

Levinas makes a similar point in examining the question of the question. Academic questioning generally addresses some aspect of being and can therefore be seen as belonging to the realm of ontology. However, Levinas asks why ask a question at all unless it is at some level a request for an answer from an other?

This latter example illustrates that Levinas sometimes uses a method akin to deconstruction of ontology in order to locate ethics secreted within the language of ontology. Thus, he argues that:

... the ego (moi) which is already declaring and affirming itself (s'affirme) – or making itself firm (s'affermit) – in being, still remains ambiguous or enigmatic enough to recognise itself as hateful, to use Pascal's term, in this very manifestation of its emphatic identity of its ipseity, in the 'saying I'. The superb priority of A = A, the principle of intelligibility and meaning [it is worth noting that Leibniz identified A = A as the law of identity], this sovereignty, or freedom within the human ego, is also, as it were, the moment when humility occurs. This questions the affirmation and strengthening of being found in the famous and facilely rhetorical quest for the meaning of life, which suggests that the absolute ego, already endowed with meaning by its vital, psychic and social forces, or its transcendental sovereignty, then returned to its mauvaise conscience. (Levinas in Hand (ed.), 1989: 81)

Levinas examines the discourse of the ego's affirmation, locates the undecidable element of humility in Pascal's self-hating I and moves on to locate the ego's radical alterity, its *mauvaise conscience*. This is perhaps the clearest indication of how inescapable the ethical impulse is. Even as one's ego affirms itself, one's *mauvaise conscience* niggles in the background about one's responsibilities.

The latter example also reveals an affinity within Levinasian ethics for deconstruction. Critchley argues that deconstruction incorporates an ethical moment in the Levinasian sense in the following way:

The ethical moment that motivates deconstruction is this Yes-saying to the unnameable, a moment of unconditional affirmation that is addressed to an alterity that can neither be excluded from nor included within logocentric conceptuality. (Critchley, 1992: 41)

Thus, the moral element of deconstruction lies in the identification of alterity, which takes the form of an affirmation of the other in philosophical discourse. The irreducibility of alterity and the consequent unconditionality of its affirmation leads Derrida to assert that ' ... unconditionality ... defines the injunction that prescribes deconstruction' (Derrida, 1988: 153). On this basis, Critchley argues that 'an unconditional categorical imperative [in the Kantian sense] or moment of affirmation is the source of the injunction that produces deconstruction' (1992: 41). It can be seen how this affirmation to the philosophical other parallels Levinas' formulation of ethics as taking responsibility and being for the other.

The above analysis indicates how Levinasian ethics can provide a strong imperative to engage in development and aid donation with a view to helping others in the South. Acceptance of the moral impulse is not inevitable, but there are strong reasons for accepting it, including its role in establishing self-identification and its manifestation as a constituting element in universal human characteristics such as language and the capacity for questioning. Critchley's identification of the affirmation of alterity (by means of deconstruction) as the product of a categorical imperative underlines the power of the moral injunction to 'be for the other'.

It might also seem that Critchley's use of such a concept indicates a resort to foundationalism that fundamentally conflicts with the deconstructive enterprise. Critchley explains his use of the 'categorical imperative' in terms of a relationship of alterity between 'hypothetical' and 'categorical' imperatives. In Kantian terms a hypothetical imperative is valid inasmuch as it is a means to an end. Thus, it is conditioned by the desires of human beings and gives rise to 'prudential' maxims that have relative validity, as with Critchley's example that 'my desire for happiness is conditional upon the pursuit of some "good" – for example, riches, knowledge, long life, or health' (1992: 40). On the other hand, categorical imperatives invoke 'actions that are entirely good in themselves and are not performed for some ulterior end' (Critchley, 1992: 40). Consequently, they are unconditional and must always be obeyed. Critchley comments on his juxtaposition of imperatives as follows:

> ... for Derrida, the ethical moment is the interruption of the general context of conditioned hypothetical imperatives by an unconditional categorical imperative. Ethics arises in and as the undecidable yet determinate articulation of these two orders. (Critchley, 1992: 40)

In this way the categorical imperative manifests itself as a part of alterity. Ethics can be seen as a product of 'differance' and the categorical imperative as one half of an undecidable diarchy rather than as an unchallenged universalist moral principle.

Like deconstruction, Levinasian ethics does not try to establish founding principles. As Cohen puts it 'its "essence", so to speak, is precisely not to have an essence, to unsettle essences' (Levinas, 1985: 10). All this suggests that there is a coincidence between Levinasian ethics and deconstruction, in that both act to displace that which is privileged and to affirm the other. It might be suggested that Levinasian ethics provides a strong (if ontologically unfounded) basis for a 'deconstructive' development strategy.

However, Critchley posits a difficulty standing in the way of any deconstructive praxis. Essentially, his reading of deconstruction is a politically quietist one. To the extent that deconstruction leads us to identify an element of undecidability between concepts, or options, it would seem to make it at least problematic as to how to decide between them. He puts the question as follows:

> ... how is one to account for the move from undecidability to the political decision to combat that domination [of the privileged concept in a binary pairing]? If deconstruction is the strictest possible determination of undecidability in the limitless context of, for want of a better word, experience, then this entails a suspension of the moment of decision. Yet, decisions have to be taken. But how? And in virtue of what? How does one make a decision in an undecidable terrain? I would claim ... that an adequate account of the decision is essential to the possibility of politics, and that it is precisely this that deconstruction does not provide. (Critchley, 1992: 199–200)

Critchley goes on to suggest that an answer to this problem can be provided by reference to Levinas' account of how the one-to-one ethical relationship is mediated into the political relationship with all the others. He refers back to Levinas' view that the question of the question (or the need to question) is born in the ethical relationship to the other. However, he notes that this relationship only becomes troubled and problematic with the entry of the third party. Thus, questioning is not born of the primal ethical relationship of two, but within the community. This does not denote a chronological development as we are all born into communities. As Levinas puts it, 'the others concern me from the first'. What Levinas is denoting is that it is with the entry of the third that the question is born, complicating what would otherwise have been a straightforward one way ethical relationship to the other. The third sets a limit to responsibility (it is impossible to be infinitely responsible for two others) and this gives rise to the question of justice. Levinas writes of justice:

> Justice is necessary, that is, comparison, coexistence, contemporaneousness, assembling, order, the visibility of faces, and thus intentionality and the intellect, the intelligibility of a system, and thence also a co-presence on an equal footing as before a court of justice. (Levinas, 1981: 157)

In this way Levinas makes it clear that justice is a product of intentionality, that is ontology, with a system of laws and penalties for breach of those laws. Society, or the polis, is based on this alterity of unlimited ethical obligation tempered by justice, which places each of us on an equal footing. From ethics we derive our duties, whilst justice affords us our rights under the terms of the law.

Justice enables us to make judgements about the other in accordance with the laws of the polis. However, justice's alterity ensures that the law must be tempered with ethical care for the other so that tyrannical laws and judgements will be avoided. As Critchley puts it:

> Injustice – not to mention racism, nationalism, and imperialism – begins when one loses sight of the transcendence of the Other, and forgets that the State, with its institutions, is informed by the proximity of my relation to the Other. (Critchley, 1992: 233)

What kind of polis would express this alterity? Ontology would have to prevail to the extent that law and order was maintained, these being two basic requirements for the continued functioning of a community. However, ethics would require that the community remain open to the other, to other beliefs, to difference. Critchley argues that democracy best expresses this alterity inasmuch as it is 'an ethically grounded form of political life which is continually being called into question by asking of its legitimacy and the legitimacy of its practices and its institutions: what is justice?' (Critchley, 1992: 239). Central to this process is the practice of holding freely contested elections for the main positions of political power. Power and rulership are present, but they are contested. It should be noted that an aspect of openness is that most, if not all existing democracies might be made more open, suggesting that no existing regime may claim ultimate wisdom as to how such a system should be run.

Clearly, ethics obliges us to render assistance to the other, but an ethically informed justice enables us to distinguish which others we ought to help as against those that do not deserve our help. We can even begin to derive principles on which to base aid strategies and interventions, notably that they should be open to the differences of the other rather than imposing Northern organisational systems, values, and hierarchies. However, it is not as easy as that. Not too long after Critchley published his book, Derrida expressed severe doubts about efforts to invest deconstruction with an ethical significance. He commented that he preferred to deny an ethics, thus giving

> ammunition to the officials of anti-deconstruction, but all in all I prefer that to the constitution of a consensual euphoria or, worse a community of complacent deconstructionists, reassured and reconciled with the world in ethical certainty, good conscience, satisfaction of service rendered, and the consciousness of duty accomplished, (or, more heroically still, yet to be accomplished).
> (in Dronsfield and Midgley, 1997: 88)

It would seem that the prospect that particularly worried Derrida was that of an ostensibly 'deconstructionist' ethical code arising that would impose its own ontological totalising system of rules and classifications, or of 'ethical certainty'. If such a system were to emerge, it would simply impose its own closure, making its own exclusions of those cases and categories that did not fit into its established rules. Such an eventuality would be in contradiction of the essence of deconstruction, this being to identify and recognise alterity, the other.

This line of thought raises the question that has occurred to many commentators, of how one is to draw any conclusions within a deconstructionist framework. The very act of taking a decision means that one embraces a particular course and excludes all the other possible courses of action. Whatever one does, difference is in some form excluded. We are driven back to the dilemma of undecidability identified by Critchley whereby we are unable to make a decision because whatever we decide will be exclusionary. However, Derrida himself insists that any significant decision must emerge from a context of undecidability. How can undecidability constitute a necessary ground for decision when its very nature seems to suggest an inability to decide something? This question can be seen to be closely related to one of our central themes, that of the dilemma between foundationalism, which gives us a basis for making decisions at the cost of making exclusions, and relativism, which can make allowance for difference, but at the cost of invalidating our grounds for making decisions. In order to address this question we must return to make a fuller investigation of deconstruction.

4.4   A PHILOSOPHY OF THE LEAST VIOLENCE

In our initial discussion of deconstruction we saw that philosophers and linguists tend to accord speech a position of privilege in relation to writing because they regard speech as implying presence, and therefore a greater likelihood of true understanding, whereas in writing the meaning can be lost due to misinterpretation, or other accidents. Deconstruction destabilised this hierarchy with the demonstration that misunderstanding can occur with speech, thus undermining the foundational claims made in respect of speech. However, as we shall see, a lot more is going on in Derrida's examination of linguistics than this initial account suggests.

Derrida points out that Saussure, the founder of linguistics, wishes to claim that speech is more fundamental than writing, but that he also stipulates that the relation between a sign (whether it be the spoken or written word) and what it signifies is arbitrary. There is no natural relationship between the tree that we see in a park and the sign 'tree'. Nothing about the actual tree motivates us to choose the sign 'tree' to signify it. This arbitrary relationship suggests that signs are not natural, but are instituted, or imposed. We recognise a sign as denoting what it signifies because the sign can be repeated (it is iterable, as Derrida puts it) and so we learn to associate the sign with what it signifies by convention (this is something that we learn to do as children when we learn to speak). Thus, the sign (a word in our example of the tree) is instituted, whether in its written or spoken form. However, if the sign, whether written or spoken, is instituted rather than being natural, Saussure has no basis for saying that the spoken form is more natural than the written form. He has shown that both are equally unnatural. This contradiction destabilises Saussure's hierarchies.

Derrida proposes the category of arche-writing, which includes both written and spoken speech, to denote that both writing and speech have common characteristics. Both types of signs (whether written or spoken) are instituted rather than being natural, they must be iterable (that is they must be repeatable) so that their meaning (what they signify) can be learned, and they also carry the same possibility for being misunderstood. It may be remembered from Chapter 2 that the term 'arche' denotes an origin. Saussure was trying to suggest that speech was prior to writing by arguing that the latter represented an imperfect adaptation of the former inasmuch as writing was less effective at accurately conveying meaning than the more original speech. Derrida undermines this argument, somewhat ironically implying that his category must be more original than both since it consists of the characteristics common to both speech and writing. This may be deemed ironic to the extent that it is impossible to determine the origin of signs and language, whether written or spoken. However, arche-writing can lay claim to an originary status of sorts, not only in comprising of the common characteristics of signs, but also in that those characteristics – institution, iterability, and the possibility for misinterpretation – are all essential for signs to perform their task of conveying meaning.

It may seem strange to argue that the possibility for misinterpretation is in some way necessary if signs are to convey meaning. However, this is precisely what Derrida argues. He points out that signs have to be iterable, which means that they have to be used in different contexts. The nuances of meaning of a sign will vary from one context to another, and with that comes the structural possibility of misinterpretation. Even if we use exactly the same sign in exactly the same context on two different occasions, there is not absolute identity between the two uses of the sign because it has been used at two different times. In other words, a sign must be iterable to have identity, or meaning, but this same iterability undercuts identity because absolute repetition, that is repetition without any difference from the initial occasion of use (even if one can identify such an occasion), is impossible. Derrida's point is that the very words we use to communicate incorporate identity, but also manifest alterity in that repetition destabilises identity.

At this stage it can be observed that Derrida's analysis goes beyond simply destabilising conceptual hierarchies (although that is certainly a part of what deconstruction does). However, it would be wrong to argue that he is in fact undermining the conditions of linguistic meaning. Rather, one can argue that he is investigating the conditions under which we establish meaning, and the costs that we incur through this process. We have to use instituted signs to denote concepts, phenomena, and build conceptual structures, but the repetition necessary to give those signs meaning, or identity, also destabilises that identity. This double-edged process informs all our efforts to institute knowledge, to define concepts and categories. For example, Saussure made a decision to follow established philosophical conceptual hierarchies in privileging speech over writing and justified it by asserting that this was a natural decision. However, Derrida's demonstration that the exclusion of writing is artificial indicates that Saussure's decision involved a loss of meaning, an exclusion of alterity. This exclusion manifests itself as the contradiction that Derrida locates in Saussure's arguments (he asserts that no signs are natural, but then tells us that speech is more natural than writing). This contradiction is the 'trace' of alterity. In a sense the excess of Saussure's arguments, his exclusions, have returned to haunt his theory, pointing up its inconsistencies. Derrida often uses the metaphor of the spectre to denote the way in which the excess of an argument, its exclusions, return to destabilise, or haunt it.

It is worth noting here that Derrida is not trying to say that we must avoid making decisions for fear of imposing exclusions. Decisions like the one that faced Saussure are necessary and unavoidable for there to be meaning and knowledge. No analytical position or decision can avoid making exclusions. We have already seen that the signs we use to signify concepts and phenomena are invested with meaning, and simultaneously destabilised, through iteration, thus losing elements of meaning in the same gesture through which their meaning is shaped. If this is the primary structural reason that explains the inevitability of exclusions, it should also be noted that there are a number of nuances of exclusion through which this fundamental tendency can manifest itself. For example, it is impossible to gather all the relevant information pertaining to particular decisions (this being one of the main criticisms made of synoptic, or rational decision-making procedures), or to consider all possible outcomes (at least in any remotely complex scenario, which would certainly include most developmental contexts). It is also worth remembering that deliberate exclusions will almost certainly be made, either because the analyst genuinely believes a factor to be irrelevant, or because s/he wishes to misdirect the reader or hearer. Irrespective of whether exclusions are made consciously, or unconsciously, honestly or dishonestly, it is certain that exclusions will be made. All of our knowledge is established through a pattern whereby arguments and proofs that are deemed to be relevant are put forward, whilst other arguments and proofs are excluded (perhaps because they are not available to us at the time that the argument is being formulated, or because they are judged to be irrelevant). This argument is quite unlike that of Foucault, who became confused as to whether the knowledge propounded through discourse constituted truth or merely the diktat of the powerful (although we may remember that Visker was moving in the direction of a deconstructive position with the perception that discourse that recognises its exclusions is preferable to that which conceals them). For Derrida limits must be instituted and exclusions made for knowledge to be constituted at all. The ever-present possibility that such exclusions may return to destabilise the knowledge that we have won does not undermine the status of knowledge in itself.

This means that deconstruction can better explain such phenomena as scientific progress than relativist forms of postmodernism, which would describe a discipline such as Physics as one explanatory structure among many, all of equal validity. A Derridian view can accommodate both the truth claims of science, validated by rigorous analysis and experimental findings, and the inevitability that such truths will make exclusions that will return to force revisions, generating new truth claims. Thus Newtonian physics gives way to Einsteinian physics.

This exposition of deconstruction indicates that the trace has a more complex function than simply indicating the destabilising presence of a repressed alterity in a proposition. As Beardsworth puts it:

> ... the instituted trace accounts for these three moments; first, the foundation of a disciplinary space; second, its constitutive exclusions; and, third, the return of that which is excluded, within the disciplinary space. All three moments are effects of arche-writing; they together constitute what Derrida calls in 'Violence and metaphysics' an 'economy of violence'. (Beardsworth, 1996: 13)

Thus, the trace involves the decision that creates knowledge and in the same movement makes exclusions, which also leads to the return of the excluded to destabilise the constituted knowledge. All this is caused by arche-writing, which institutes signs that then undergo reiteration, a process that simultaneously invests them with identity, whilst also destabilising that identity. It is important to note that this process involves violence. In the sense that the decision that constitutes knowledge is also necessarily a decision that makes exclusions it is violent. As we have already noted, such violence is necessary for us to have knowledge. However, the extent of the violence can vary according to the status that we give our decisions – and this is what Derrida is indicating when he refers to an 'economy of violence'. In order to explain the economy of violence we must further unpack the implications of arche-writing and the limit between knowledge and its exclusions.

When we draw a limit and decide that what falls within that limit constitutes knowledge, how are we to regard that knowledge? Does it constitute absolute truth as against which all else is false, cast into doubt? Or should it be regarded as the best account that we can render at the time, but one that will be subject to revision in due time? Derrida's argumentation would clearly suggest the latter answer, given that what is excluded will return (if not in one form, then in another) and put our account into doubt. However, the central ontological tradition is one of attempts to found total accounts of being, such as those of Kant and Hegel, who both, in radically different ways, tried to provide analyses that would constitute total theories of the human condition (consequently Derrida tends to refer to this type of analysis as ontologising, or totalising). Of course Derrida would argue that, notwithstanding the genius of Kant and Hegel, the nature of arche-writing dooms such enterprises from the start. As we have repeatedly observed, iteration establishes identity, but at the same time destabilises identity. This means that any attempt to identify a pure concept, or achieve some sort of ultimate society, is impossible because 'its condition of possibility is also its condition of impossibility' (this is a formulation that Derrida often uses). The concept must be repeated to give it meaning and this is its condition of possibility, but that repetition also puts its meaning into question, this being its condition of impossibility. Consequently, it is impossible to attain an absolutely pure principle or concept and apply it in real life.

Beardsworth provides a demonstration of this in his analysis of Kant's use of the idea of sovereignty. He notes that Kant appeals to the sovereignty of the general will as a regulative principle in politics, but eschews any appeal to full popular sovereignty due to his awareness of its potential for leading to a politics of terror (like the terror of the French Revolution). Thus Kant is endeavouring to avoid the potential for political terror in his philosophy. However, in his examination of the individual sovereign will Kant notes that the position of sovereign implies possession of rights without commitment to any duties. Beardsworth argues that Kant implies that 'no one can pretend to the position of the Sovereign since that position has ... rights but no duties'. Having recognised the danger of despotism at the individual level, Kant fails to recognise this danger at the level of political institutions. Beardsworth points out that fear of such a danger prompted the emergence of the principle of separation of powers, although this is something Kant seems not to grasp. Beardsworth continues:

> The legislative is not simultaneously the executive because full sovereignty – what Rousseau in the Social Contract calls 'true democracy' in which the governed are also the governors (1762: III, Chapter IV) – would mean the end of the relation to the other. If one has no duty to others, then the social relation has come to an end. The logical and historical consequence is the non-recognition of the other (whether this be in the form of ignorance, forgetting or murder). *True democracy* is thus *the death of democracy*. (1996: 66)

If a polity claims full sovereignty, it is claiming that nobody is politically excluded and that in this sense there is no other. Any who are in fact excluded (for example, new social, or political groupings that emerge over a period of time) will not be recognised and consequently will be repressed. In this sense, the society that attempts to legislate full democracy can never attain that goal. Pure democracy cannot be achieved. The attempt to do so will result in an undemocratic situation, the death of democracy as Beardsworth dramatically puts it.

Similar lines of thought can be developed with regard to such concepts as freedom, or rights, where it can be seen that if the freedom or rights of one (whether a grouping, or an individual) are taken to their logical conclusion, the freedom or rights of others will be infringed. The central point here is that if we try to institute closure, if we try to legislate a 'true' democracy, or true freedom, we will inevitably fail. This will leave us with an undemocratic society masquerading as a democracy, concealing its exclusions and concomitant injustice. It will result in violence. As we have seen, any decision is violent. However, when we try to achieve a closure in the form of making a claim to being a truly democratic, or truly free society, we bring about more violence in the form of repression of the excluded. Consequently, we should try to avoid what Derrida might term 'ontologisation', closure in the form of a claim to have achieved the ideal. If we suspend the promise of a perfect democracy, regarding it as a future aim that will never actually be achieved, we leave open the option to revise our democratic rules, which gives us the opportunity to respond to the others who have been excluded. By avoiding closure, by acknowledging that we shall have to return to the problem of the other, of alterity, again and again – in this way we achieve the lesser violence. It is for this reason that Derrida refers to deconstruction as a philosophy of the lesser violence.

4.5   UNDECIDABILITY AND THE DECISION

So far we have seen that arche-writing operates to destabilise identity at the same time it establishes it. This process is part of the economy of violence through which arche-writing makes violent exclusions as a part of establishing identity, exclusions that return to destabilise that identity. Consequently, attempts to totalise are bound to fail and, to the extent that we try to disguise this failure, we enhance the violence caused by our theories. This is already suggestive of a particular political and moral stance of openness to change, receptiveness to the other, a course of less violence.

However, to the extent that an ethics is reflected in this formulation it is rather different from the ethics of Levinas. In the first place, it would seem that for Derrida the relationship to the other is always tainted with an inescapable violence from the beginning. As Hobson puts it:

> Against Levinas' demand for total respect for the other in its otherness, Derrida urges that to speak of the other as other cannot, by its very nature, be done elsewhere than from the other's 'appearance for me'; in that way, it has to make the other subsidiary to my viewpoint – and thus does not conserve it respectfully in its otherness. (1998: 36)

As we saw earlier, Levinas sees language as being born out of respect for the other, whereas Derrida sees language as intrinsically violent in its function of allocating meaning by way of defining, categorising and excluding. This would seem to suggest that a deconstructionist ethics would be less an ethics of '*total*' respect for the other and more of an ethics of the least violence.

Beardsworth also differentiates between deconstruction and Levinasian ethics, arguing that Levinas develops a particularist ethics that would have to be seen as departing from the moral principle of the lesser violence from a Derridian point of view. This critique of Levinas starts with the observation that the deconstructionist concept of alterity cannot be figured, that is to say that we cannot forecast the form that the excluded, the other, will take. The others might be human, but they could just as easily be animals, other species, that are maltreated and excluded by humankind. Alterity is not given a form by Derrida. However, for Levinas it is. The other is always human, and Beardsworth argues that Levinas' view of twentieth-century history motivates him to specify even further. Particularly during the twentieth century the Jewish people can be seen as having been cast in the role of Europe's brutally repressed other. This motivates Levinas to observe that the 'authentically human' is the 'being-Jewish in every man'. One need not take up an anti-Jewish position, or ignore the extreme violence of the Holocaust, to observe that Levinas' formulation is itself exclusionary and violent. The partiality of his view becomes evident when he identifies Zionism as 'the promise of a future of the other'. Zionism as practised by the state of Israel would appear to hold out a particularly bleak promise of a future for the other if we think of that other not as a Jew, but as a Palestinian Muslim (Beardsworth, 1996: 140–4). Clearly, such considerations must give us pause in considering the applicability of a Levinasian ethics, but as we shall see, they do not strip it of all value in Derrida's eyes.

If these observations create problems for Critchley's proposed fusion of deconstruction with Levinasian ethics, we have yet to deal with the other main problem posed by his thesis (or rather, Derrida's criticism of it), that of how a decision can arise (indeed, must arise) from a situation of undecidability. We shall now turn to this issue, which will also illustrate how the process of making a decision on the basis of undecidability brings both politics and ethics into play. In a strategy that will be familiar to the reader we shall approach this issue by an indirect route, considering Derrida's use of aporia, and in particular, what might be termed the aporia of law.

Beardsworth provides quite a full account of Derrida's use of aporia, or aporetics. He notes that the pre-Socratic sophists 'called an aporia two contradictory sayings of equal value' (1996: 32). Since the two sayings cannot be reconciled with each other, the proper response to them was deemed to be a suspension of judgement. In other words one cannot work with the two sayings to combine them and produce a satisfactory and full synthesis, or outcome. Aporia is reminiscent of the Hegelian dialectic in that it consists of two opposed factors or values but, unlike the dialectic, the two values cannot be reconciled. In his use of aporia Derrida is consciously departing from Hegelian philosophy, which totalises by arguing that all history is characterised by a teleological dialectical process in which contradictory forces combine to produce synthesis, all of which leads to a final complete synthesis (the *aufhebung*) in which all contradictions are reconciled. Derrida, of course, rejects the suggestion that a closure can be accomplished that will not be exclusionary, and consequently rejects Hegelian dialectical contradiction in favour of aporetic contradiction in which there can be no reconciliation of contradictory forces, and consequently no closure.

However, Derrida's use of aporia is also different from its usage in classical philosophy. Whereas for the Greeks an aporia denoted two contradictory sayings, or factors, for Derrida 'the "contradiction" applies to one and the same entity, not to two different entities' (Beardsworth, 1996: 32). In the last section we saw that any sign has to be iterable, repeatable, to be invested with meaning, or identity. However, the very same process of iteration destabilises meaning at the same time that it establishes it. This is an aporetic process inasmuch as two contradictory trends are emerging from the same process of iteration. The identity of a sign is being established at the same time as it is put into doubt. Its condition of possibility is also its condition of impossibility.

Derrida examines the manifestations of this aporetic process at a variety of levels in a number of concepts, notably including the law (considered both in terms of legal systems and in terms of laws of how things work). One manifestation of the aporia of law concerns the law's origin, or lack of an easily discernible origin. Indeed, if meaning is constituted through repetition it would follow that there can be no easily identifiable singular occasion that we can locate as the time when law was founded. Derrida illustrates this point in at least two contexts that we can draw on, the first concerning the mythical foundation of law recounted in Freud's *Totem and Taboo*. A much abbreviated version of the latter account would note that the story concerns a group of sons who are jealous of their father's power and consequently kill him. This parricide so strikes them with remorse that they set up a totem to substitute the father and institute laws against killing the totem. The point that Derrida makes is that this does not explain the origin of law at all because the moral law against parricide would already have to be in place for the sons to be remorseful about their 'crime'. Thus, origins prove elusive at the level of myth. It would seem that one aspect of the aporia of law is that, as Beardsworth puts it, 'the origin of law does not take place and does not not take place' (Beardsworth, 1996: 30–35).

A similar point can be made with regard to the factual example of the American Declaration of Independence. This historical event could indeed be seen as an identifiable moment when a nation and its legal system were founded. However, even this event becomes problematic if we seek to classify it as a foundation of law. For at the time that the Declaration was signed its signatories were breaking the law, the colonial law that they had hitherto accepted. As Derrida notes:

> There was no signatory, by right, before the text of the Declaration which remains itself the producer and the guarantor of its own signature. (in Bennington, 2000: 29)

Derrida goes on to argue that the Declaration represents a '*coup de force*' that 'makes right, founds right, gives right, *gives rise to the law*' (as above). Aporia manifests itself here as a founding of law that is itself illegal, a *coup de force*. This reflects the violence that occurs in the investment of a sign with meaning, which is at the same time exclusory. In this sense any founding action must be violent. Even a foundation of law will involve an element of violence and illegality.

Bennington also notes that the American Declaration of Independence is a site of undecidability. The signatories of the Declaration refer to themselves as the 'Representatives of the United States of America', acting 'by the authority of the good people of these Colonies' (in Beardsworth, 1996: 99). As Bennington observes, the United States as a nation, with a people to represent as a national people, only comes into existence with the signing of the Declaration. Yet throughout the Declaration it refers to the United States and its people as already existing. The element of undecidability is 'between the sense that the declaration *describes* a state of affairs (e.g. a state of affairs that already exists) and the sense that it *produces* the state of affairs it appears to describe' (Bennington, 2000: 29). It can be seen that this situation of undecidability is simply a different way of viewing the aporia of law as developed above. The wording of the Declaration is such as to suggest that the foundation of the United

States does not take place (because it already seems to exist according to the Declaration), but it does not not take place because the signatories are putting their names to a founding document. This might be seen as a reinscription of aporia as undecidability.

Having seen how closely interrelated aporia and undecidability are (indeed, they might be regarded as the same phenomenon, but viewed from different angles), we can now proceed to see how aporia and undecidability set the context for the decision. Again, we shall work with the example of the law. We are now well aware of the way that arche-writing invests identity whilst making exclusions that return to haunt the identity created. It follows from this that no law can be perfect in its coverage. An excess in the form of singular cases that do not fit the categories set up by law will return to haunt the law, thus necessitating further judgements. The law is supposed to be general in its coverage of society, applying to all of us as individual members of society. However, it cannot account for each individual's, even each group's, circumstances, and so cases will arise that are anomalous, that will require further judgement. Indeed, this has to happen for there to be judgement. If judgement really could totalise so that it could cover every possible set of circumstances there would be no need for judgement. A perfect set of laws would have been produced to cover every eventuality and all that would need to be done would be to apply the rules for each case as it arose. The impossibility of successful totalisation, and the consequent inevitability of the emergence of singular cases, is what makes judgement necessary. This explains why judgement must take place in a situation of undecidability. The aporetic nature of arche-writing manifests itself in the law as an inability to produce laws that will be general in their coverage in the sense of covering every conceivable eventuality that might come before the law. Consequently, when an eventuality occurs that the law has failed to anticipate, the need for judgement arises in a situation where there are no applicable rules to guide decision-making. A judgement must be made in an undecidable terrain in at least two senses. Firstly, if we merely had to follow the rules in adjudicating a particular case, this would not involve judgement, just mechanical adherence to the rules. Secondly, the necessity of making judgements on undecidable cases means that we will inevitably produce judgements that make exclusions, thus creating the conditions for the emergence of further singular cases that will demand judgement. It is particularly in the latter sense that judgements, or decisions must emerge from a situation of undecidability.

The second point also shows that this is a situation that will continue to reproduce itself again and again. This might be illustrated by presenting the decision-making process as a number of steps. Firstly, an anomalous case comes before the law, which does not fit into the categories established by law, and so it demands judgement in a context of undecidability. Secondly, judgement will be made on the case in question that will inevitably be violent in terms of making its own exclusions. Thirdly, these exclusions will result in yet further anomalies that require yet more judgements and so on. This indicates how undecidability and judgement are interlinked in an ongoing dynamic process, with judgement and its concomitant exclusions leading to anomalous, or undecidable cases, which in turn demand further judgements. The situation is unending. It is for this reason that politics has an unending horizon for deconstructionists.

At this point we can bring politics and ethics back into our analysis. Derrida notes that the violence concomitant in judgement concerns politics:

> ... once it is granted that violence is in fact irreducible, it becomes necessary – and this is the moment of politics – to have rules, conventions and stabilizations of power. (in Mouffe, 1996: 83)

It is clear from this statement that politics and ethics are interlinked for Derrida in that politics is about controlling power, stipulating rules and conventions to limit abuse of power. The extent of this co-implication of ethics and politics becomes particularly evident in the following statement:

> Every time that I hear someone say that 'I have taken a decision', or 'I have assumed my responsibilities', I am suspicious because if there is responsibility or decision one cannot determine them as such or have certainty or good conscience with regard to them. If I conduct myself particularly well with regard to someone, I know that it is to the detriment of an other; of one nation to the detriment of another nation, of one family to the detriment of another family, of my friends to the detriment of other friends or non-friends, etc. This is the infinitude that inscribes itself within responsibility; otherwise there would be no ethical problems or

decisions. And this is why undecidability is not a moment to be traversed and overcome. Conflicts of duty – and there is only duty in conflict – are interminable and even when I take my decision and do something, undecidability is not at an end. I know that I have not done enough and it is in this way that morality continues, that history and politics continue. There is politicisation or ethicization because undecidability is not simply a moment to be overcome by the occurrence of the decision. Undecidability continues to inhabit the decision and the latter does not close itself off from the former. The relation to the other does not close itself off, and it is because of this that there is history and one tries to act politically. (in Mouffe, 1996: 86–7)

This typically complex paragraph tells us a great deal about how Derrida combines the issues of undecidability, the decision, politics and ethics. It confirms what we have already noted about the ongoing relationship between undecidability and the decision, where decisions take place under conditions of undecidability, therefore making exclusions, which inevitably return to demand more decisions. A clear political implication of this is that whatever decision one takes, exclusions will be made, some will benefit while others will not. Obviously, this touches on an issue at the heart of politics, distribution of resources. As Derrida clearly indicates this is also, inevitably, an ethical issue. To the extent that all our decisions reward certain groups and ignore or penalise other groups, we bear responsibility for them. This responsibility is referred to in terms that are very reminiscent of Levinas inasmuch as it is infinite. However, this point is given a Derridian twist in that, whereas for Levinas infinite responsibility was a reaction to the existence of the other, Derrida locates that responsibility in our decisions and the way that they inevitably disadvantage or exclude an other.

The latter point brings in the issue of the third party in the ethical relationship, but in a rather different way to that developed by Critchley. It may be remembered that Critchley uses the third party to solve what he saw as the problem of undecidability, arguing after Levinas that the third brings in the question of justice. This enables us to calculate what is fair to all the parties involved in a decision, thus enabling us to make a judgement. We can now see that what Derrida would object to in this is the implication that a final decision might be possible, one that makes no exclusions. In other words there is an element of totalisation in this thesis. In fairness to

Critchley, it should be noted that he does stipulate that there can never be a perfectly just polis, thus preserving the notion that our political responsibility is unending. However, he does not trace this responsibility to its locus in our decisions and their exclusory nature as determined by undecidability.

In contrast to Critchley's account, Derrida sees the third party as bringing in the issue of justice in the following way:

> The third party does not wait, his illeity calls from the moment of epiphany of the face in the face-to-face. For the absence of the third party would threaten with violence the purity of the ethical in the absolute immediacy of the face-to-face with the unique. No doubt Levinas does not say it in this form. But what is he doing when, beyond or through the duel of the face-to-face between two 'unique beings', he appeals to justice, affirms and reaffirms that justice 'is necessary' [il faut]? Is he not, then, taking into account this hypothesis of a violence of pure and immediate ethics in the face-to-face of the face? Of a violence potentially unleashed in the experience of the neighbour and of absolute uniqueness? Of the impossibility of discerning good from evil, love from hatred, giving from taking, desire for life and death drive, hospitable welcome from selfish or narcissistic enclosure?
>
> The third party would thus protect against the vertigo of ethical violence itself. Ethics could be doubly exposed to this same violence: exposed to suffer it, but also to exercise it. Alternatively or simultaneously. It is true that the protective or mediating third party, in its juridico-politico becoming, in turn violates, at least virtually, the purity of the ethical desire for the unique. Whence the terrifying fatality of a double constraint. (Derrida, 1997: 32–3)

In this passage Derrida is moulding Levinas' observations on the third party in such a way that they fit with a deconstructionist position (hence 'Levinas does not say it in this form'). What Derrida is arguing here is that, contrary to anything Levinas explicitly said, the ethical relationship of two, the face-to-face, could be a source of violence. If our responsibility to the other is infinite it follows that if the other inflicts violence on us we should submit to it. Similarly, if the other requires us to inflict violence on yet others we should obey. Obviously, either of these outcomes is fatal to Levinas' project of developing an ethical philosophy. Consequently, Derrida argues that the presence of the third party, who is there right from the beginning, guards against such an outcome by introducing justice. Levinas notes that justice entails rules, laws, and calculation of our obligations to all the others, not just the other of what he terms the face-to-face. Indeed, justice means that the law will protect us from any unjust abuse by the other. This prevents violence emerging from the face-to-face.

However, Derrida also notes that the presence of the third from the beginning introduces a contradiction into the Levinasian ethical relationship to the other. If the third represents the claims of justice right from the beginning of the face-to-face this violates the ethical relationship based on our responsibility to the other. I cannot be *infinitely* responsible to the other whilst recognising any claims by a third. This is the double constraint that Derrida mentions at the end of the passage. Ethics is founded in the relation to the other, but it is necessarily violated from the beginning by the presence of the third, whose presence is essential to prevent violence emerging from the face-to-face. It is this move in Derrida's argument that alerts us as to how he is adapting Levinasian ethics to a deconstructive position. The founding of ethics is violated from the beginning. Its identity is established and destabilised by the presence of the third. The third is excluded from the original Levinasian formulation of the ethical relation to the other, but is also necessary to prevent that relation descending into a violence that would destroy its ethical nature. We can present this idea in two familiar aporetic, or undecidable formulations. Firstly, the presence of the third is both the condition of possibility of ethics and its condition of impossibility. Secondly, the foundation of ethics is based on a violation of ethics (the presence of the third) in the same way that the foundation of American law in the American Declaration of Independence was founded in a violation of law. It is also worth noting once again how inextricably Derrida interlinks the ethical and the political by involving the third in ethics from the beginning. Whereas Critchley brought in the question of the third contingently, to solve what he thought was the problem of undecidability, Derrida argues that ethics and politics are intertwined from the beginning.

That ethics is founded with a violation, just as American law is founded with a breach of the law, shows how inescapable violence is. The pursuit of a pure ethics leads to violence, just as we saw that the ideal of a pure freedom was also violent in the final analysis. This means that violence, the intervention of the third, is essential to prevent a worse violence emerging from the pure ethical relationship of the face-to-face. In the same way, the violence of the law is necessary to prevent the worse violence implied by complete freedom of the individual. Whatever choice we make, whatever arguments we advance, we necessarily make exclusions, we engage in violence. This shows just how heavy our responsibility is to make the decision of the least violence.

Bennington points up an interesting consideration in relation to the latter argument inasmuch as it entails a danger of becoming decisionistic. What he means by this is that it seems to put the emphasis on a traditionally conceived subject (what we have referred to as the 'over-determined subject') bearing responsibility for all decisions. Bennington arrives at this position by noting that a violence is necessary to ethics to prevent worse violence. As he puts it:

> ... ethics in this Levinasian sense can be made coherent only by allowing that it protect itself from itself by a necessarily risky innoculatory contamination of itself by its apparent other(s). In this sense Derrida will say that ethics is essentially *pervertible*, and that this pervertibility is the positive condition (to be affirmed, then) of all the positive values (the Good, the Just, and so on) ethics enjoins us to seek. (Bennington, 2000: 42)

As we saw earlier, an essential aspect of arche-writing is that the sign can be misunderstood, the alterity that is excluded from it returns to destabilise identity. So, with ethics, the violence that is attendant at its birth (the intrusion of the third in the face-to-face), but which is excluded from the concept, can return to pervert ethics. Consequently, as Bennington argues, we know that ethics can be perverted, but we cannot know in advance just when it is going to happen. Without a grounded ethical code that stipulates just what is right and wrong and guides us what to do, 'it looks unavoidable that ethics come(s) to be a matter of singular decisions taken on the occasion of singular events' (Bennington: 2000: 43). Herein lies the danger of conceiving ethics as the province of the over-determined subject deciding what is right and wrong for him- or herself.

Bennington argues that the corrective to this tendency is provided by Derrida's conception that decisions take place through the 'other in me'. This seems to refer back to the Levinasian idea that our individuality, our self-identity is formed in relation to the other. Derrida radicalises this idea and throws a deconstructionist light on it, asserting 'can one not claim ... that without exonerating me in any way, decision and responsibility are always of the other? That they always come back down to the other, from the other, be it the other in me?' (in Bennington, 2000: 44). We have already observed that decision takes place in a situation of undecidability, by definition a situation in which alterity, the exclusions of our previous decisions, have come back to haunt us, demanding a further decision. In this sense our decisions always concern the other. However, the idea of the 'other in me' is suggestive of the process by which our own individual identities have been formed, in large part through social-isation by others. The individual core of us, what we call 'I', also incorporates alterity, the lasting impact on us of those who have been close to us, and who constitute the other in us. In this sense, it could be argued that any decisions we make will be made at least in part through the other(s) within us. It is this sense also that guards against us conceiving of ethics, even seen through a deconstructionist framework, as being the province of a sovereign individual subject.

Thus far we have argued that deconstruction views decision-making as taking place in a context of undecidability. Our decisions, for example about the law, make violent exclusions that return to haunt the laws we have created. Because the singularities, the cases that haunt us, do not fit with our established laws, we have to make new decisions to deal with them, which in turn will make their own violent exclusions. This violence is unavoidable, but it is our respon-sibility because we are the ones who have taken the decisions and have excluded the other, whether knowingly, or unknowingly. This is also a crucial point at which politics and ethics come into play in the shape of our political and ethical responsibility to identify and practise the decision of least violence. We have seen that this generally involves avoidance of what Derrida terms 'totalisation' or 'ontologisation', the practice of trying to pass off our ideas as a total system that provides all the answers to our problems.

But what else does it mean for politics and development? Can we identify what might characterise a politics, or development of the least violence in practice? This is a dangerous question in that we have seen Derrida's nervousness and suspicion of attempts to derive some sort of programme from his work, be it ethical, or political. Indeed, to say 'this is what deconstruction is and here is how we can use it as a basis for action' would be to fall into making exclusions that would come back to haunt us. However, that does not mean that deconstruction has no implications for action, and Derrida makes this much clear himself, notably in *Spectres of Marx*. In the next section we shall tentatively begin to explore what deconstruction might mean for action, particularly pertaining to development issues. But with a strong proviso – subject to review!

4.6   DECONSTRUCTION, POLITICS, DEVELOPMENT

Earlier in this chapter we briefly noted how Critchley argued that a politics of deconstruction would be democratic. He based this conclusion on a number of factors, notably that it is 'ethically grounded' in terms of putting its governors and system of governance into question through the electoral process, and that it is open to the other. These are still entirely valid points, notwithstanding the aforegoing revision of Critchley's view of the relationship between politics, ethics and undecidability. However, we can elaborate further on the linkages of deconstruction and democracy on the basis of Derrida's more recent writings and, particularly through an illuminating commentary by Bennington.

Bennington points out that in *The Politics of Friendship* Derrida elaborates the idea of a democracy based on the following tension:

> No democracy without respect for singularity or irreducible alterity, but no democracy without 'community of friends' (koina ta philon), without calculation of majorities, without subjects which are identifiable stabilisable, representable and equal among themselves. These two laws are irreducible to one another. Tragically irreconcilable and wounding forever. (in Bennington, 2000: 30)

The practice of democracy has to live up to these two principles, respect for each individual, and the equality of each individual before the law, which enables the polity to take votes and represent collective interests. Obviously there is a contradiction here in that, if a minority group or an individual loses a vote, then that minority, or individual, suffers an infraction, otherness is excluded. Democracy in practice inevitably entails the taking of decisions and, as we have seen, decisions inevitably exclude. If democracy is inevitably repressive in practice, why should we prefer democracy to any other political system? Derrida answers as follows:

> ... one is keeping one's right to question, to critique, to deconstruction (rights which are in principle guaranteed by every democracy: no deconstruction without democracy, no democracy

without deconstruction). One keeps this right in order to mark strategically what is no longer a matter of strategy: the limit between the conditional (the edges of the context and concept of democracy which enclose the effective practice of democracy and feed it on soil and blood) and the unconditional which, from the start, will have inscribed an auto-deconstructive force in the very motif of democracy, the possibility and the duty for democracy to de-limit itself ... A delimitation not only in the name of a regulative idea and an indefinite perfectibility, but each time in the singular urgency of a *here and now.* (in Bennington, 2000: 32)

Essentially, democracy allows us to put its working into question. By allowing us to question, democracy enables us to deconstruct it, to identify any of its exclusions of alterity in the way that it works at any given time or place, and to demand that it reform itself in the name of an open democracy that does not exclude. The above-mentioned contradiction between individual/minority rights and majority voting means that in actuality democracy can never be perfected. Consequently, democracy must remain open, it cannot institute closure, and, simultaneously, it is encouraging of a political praxis of emancipation of the excluded.

It is notable then that a central aspect of Derrida's democratic commitment is precisely that it does entail a praxis, an emancipatory praxis. As we shall see, this is in large part what Derrida finds attractive in the work of Marx. In the first instance *Spectres of Marx* reacts to the liberal triumphalism that greeted the collapse of the Soviet bloc in the early 1990s, and, in particular, deconstructs one of the central texts of the period, Fukuyama's *The End of History and the Last Man.* At this stage there is little to be gained by any further detailed examination of this much criticised and largely discredited volume. However, it is worth noting Derrida's diagnosis of the glee displayed by Fukuyama and his ilk in their declaration of the death of Marxism. He comments as follows:

This dominating discourse often has the manic, jubilatory, and incantatory form that Freud assigned to the so-called triumphant phase of the mourning work. The incantation repeats and ritualises itself, it holds forth and holds to formulas, like any animistic magic. To the rhythm of a cadenced march, it proclaims: Marx is dead, communism is dead, very dead, and along with it its hopes, its discourse, its theories, and its practices. It says: long live capitalism, long live the market, here's to the survival of economic and political liberalism! (Derrida, 1994: 51–2)

The reader may remember that when we noted that all arguments make exclusions, we also saw that some exclusions are deliberately made, indeed dishonestly made. Derrida's satire in the above passage is clearly aimed at just such an instance. The eagerness with which liberal demagogues stumbled over each other in their efforts to bury Marxism and declare the triumph of capitalism represented a very clear demonstration of a wish to deliberately exclude, to institute closure. However, this closure was not only designed to exclude Marxist theory. It was aimed at any force that might challenge the liberal consensus, a consensus that underwrites Northern market domination over the South (which might now be defined as including the ex-communist states of Eastern Europe). Henceforth, there would only be one way forward, one path to development so the liberals insisted, and that would be through their holy of holies, the free market. After all, anybody who was excluded through the market was righteously excluded, because they were economically uncompetitive. It was on this basis that the World Bank and the IMF opened up successive Southern economies to competition from the North, and ensured that Southern states paid their debts to Northern financial institutions, whilst the economies of that same North continued practising protectionism on a massive scale.

The main burden of Derrida's analysis is that neither is liberal capitalism as healthy as its advocates like to pretend it is, nor is Marxism as dead as these same liberals would like to suggest. Derrida enumerates ten 'plagues' of the liberal new world order, including many that directly affect the South. They include the growth of world unemployment in the face of economic deregulation, the exclusion of the homeless from political life, the continual economic dog-fights between the main economic players of the USA, the EU and Japan, the associated protectionist strategies of the Northern states, the continued problem of international indebtedness, the activities of the arms industry, the spread of nuclear weapons, the 'properly capitalist phantom-States that are mafia and the drug cartels on every continent, including in the former so-called socialist States of Eastern Europe' (this reference would make Derrida one of the earlier commentators to notice the emergence of the mafia as Russia's leading multinational corporation) (1994: 83), and, last but not least, the domination of the main international institutions (e.g.

the United Nations, the World Bank and the IMF) by the Northern states. All of these deformations of the international political economy make exclusions, whether at the international, or local level, whether in the North or the South. What they all have in common is that the excluded almost invariably seem to be the weakest, whether it be the weaker nations forced to take the IMF's free market medicine undiluted, or those who lose their jobs due to deregulation. Indeed, the numbers of those who are excluded rather than being uplifted by the world liberal order show every sign of being on the increase. The liberal capitalist strategy of development seems to be wearing thin within remarkably few years after its supposed triumph.

The eagerness of liberal ideologues to bury Marxism is eminently explicable in the face of these numerous exclusions in the name of capitalist development, for, as Derrida perceives, Marx was and remains par excellence a theorist and advocate of emancipation of the excluded. Derrida comments on this as follows:

> Now, if there is a spirit of Marxism that I will never be ready to renounce, it is not only the critical idea or the questioning stance … It is even more a certain emancipatory and messianic affirmation, a certain experience of the promise that one can try to liberate from any dogmatics and even from any metaphysico-religious determination, from any messianism. And a promise must promise to be kept, that is, not to remain 'spiritual' or 'abstract', but to produce events, new effective forms of action, practice, organization, and so forth. (1994: 89)

Derrida is playing on a number of senses of the word 'promise' here. He often uses the word promise to denote the excess, or exclusions of an argument or position. However, he is also playing on the sense of promise as meaning the hope that an idea or argument might seem to hold for the future. One can find references to the promise of democracy throughout Derrida's work, and it suggests that what is currently excluded from our determinations of democracy will return, but also that this return will help to achieve the promise that democracy holds for a more inclusive society. In the above passage, Derrida is making a similar point about Marxism to the effect that it holds out an emancipatory promise, but also playing on the sense of 'promise' as a promise of action, a promise to do something. Here again, Derrida affirms that it is necessary to put theory into practice.

However, it is clear also that Derrida wants to separate the emancipatory promise of Marxism from what he terms 'dogmatics', or 'metaphysico-religious determination'. Essentially, Derrida is arguing here for the abandonment of Marxian retention of the Hegelian dialectic. As we have already mentioned, Derrida sees Hegel's dialectical system as a totalising system that tries to institute closure. This tendency manifests itself in Marxist theory in the form of the teleology of the dialectical analysis of class struggle, which is seen as leading to a resolution of the dialectic (a closure) with the establishment of the perfect society, communism. It does not seem likely that many Marxists will object fundamentally to the proposition of abandoning this aspect of Marxist theory given that many of them have already quietly jettisoned this nineteenth-century, leftist version of social Darwinism.

It might be wondered what kind of praxis Derrida envisages for any present-day emancipatory movement. Derrida is not as clear as one might ideally wish on this issue, but he does refer to the emergence of a New International, identifying it as follows:

It is a link of affinity, suffering and hope, a still discreet, almost secret link, as it was around 1848 (when Marx and Engels identified the emergence of the international proletariat in The Communist Manifesto), but more and more visible, we have more than one sign of it. It is an untimely link, without status, without title, and without name, barely public, even if it is not clandestine, without contract, 'out of joint', without coordination, without party, without country, without national community (International before, across, and beyond any national determination), without co-citizenship, without common belonging to a class. The name of new International is given here to what calls to the friendship of an alliance without institution among those who, even if they no longer believe or never believed in the socialist-Marxist International, in the dictatorship of the proletariat, in the messiano-eschatological role of the universal union of the proletarians of all lands, continue to be inspired by at least one of the spirits of Marx or of Marxism (they now know that there is more than one) and in order to ally themselves, in a new, concrete, and real way, even if this alliance no longer takes the form of a party or of a workers' international, but rather of a kind of counter-conjuration, in the (theoretical and practical) critique of the state of international law, the concepts of State and nation, and so forth; in order to renew this critique, and especially to radicalise it. (1994: 85–6)

This vision of an alliance of variegated forces, distributed about the world, and united by their opposition to various aspects of liberal hegemony, could well be seen as encompassing the various projects of the new social movements, as well as offering the prospect of a more coordinated resistance to the depredations of the new world order than the post-development agenda of largely separate local emancipatory projects. Although Derrida qualifies that this New International is not based on class or a worker's international, traditional socialist movements such as worker's organisations would not thereby be denied a significant role in it. Nor would such a role be denied to those forces based in the North that opposed the exclusory practices of liberalism anywhere in the world. A number of Marxists have taken umbrage at the suggestion that such a strategy could be deemed Marxist in any sense given that this New International does not take class or party for its basis, and does not entail belief in such canonical Marxist principles as the revolutionary world role of the proletariat, and the need for a dictatorship of the proletariat. Indeed, some have characterised this as Marxism without Marxism.

However, are these changes actually so fatal to Marxist theory? The revolutionary world role of the proletariat has already been put into question by the fact that so many revolutions have actually been carried out by agrarian classes. Furthermore, any progressive movement would be ill-advised to embrace the party structures generally associated with the communist movement, namely Leninist structures, which seem to have degenerated into various forms of bureaucratic centralism whenever and wherever they have been put into operation for any length of time. Perhaps the central area of controversy concerns what some have characterised as Derrida's abandonment of the concept of class as a crucial factor in any emancipatory theory. Derrida has actually clarified his own position in the face of such accusations, noting the following passage that was published at about the same time as *Spectres of Marx*:

I believe in the gross existence of social classes, but the modernity of industrial societies (not to mention the Third World) cannot be approached, analysed, taken into account within a political strategy, starting off from a concept whose links are so loose. I had the impression that I was still seeing models for sociological and political analysis inherited if not from the nineteenth, at least from the first half of the twentieth century ... I believe that an interest in what the concept of class struggle aimed at, an interest in analysing conflicts in social forces, is still absolutely indispensable. But I'm not sure that class, as it's been inherited, is the best instrument for those activities, unless it is considerably differentiated. (in Sprinker, 1999: 237)

What this indicates is not that class is to be dismissed as irrelevant, but rather that traditional Marxist analyses need to be revised to take into account the social and class fragmentation taking place in a context of accelerating globalisation. Indeed, most Marxists accept the need for such analysis, and surely most observers would accept the need to take into account the social diversity of the South in any emancipatory development theory.

If we turn to the question of how the New International might combat the liberal hegemony, we find that Derrida suggests two interrelated strategies based on spirits of Marxism. The first might be viewed as a strategic and/or reformist position. It would entail taking a position of at least apparent acceptance of liberal canons to the effect that the free market is the path to salvation. The point of this being to draw attention to the gap between reality and the liberal ideal in order to challenge the liberal powers to deliver on their promises of development. Derrida argues that

> even within this idealist hypothesis (e.g. acceptance of the liberal idealist hypothesis), the recourse to a certain *spirit* of the Marxist critique remains urgent and will have to remain indefinitely necessary in order to denounce and reduce the gap *as much as possible*, in order to adjust 'reality' to the 'ideal' in the course of a necessarily infinite process. (1994: 86)

The prime object of this strategy is to win actual gains for the excluded, to campaign for reform of the inegalitarian aspects of the system. It is in this context that arguments for development activity and for aid to the South become central. Such reformism is always worthwhile to the extent that it leads to real gains and improvements in the standard of living for those at the base of world society.

The second strategy might be seen as an inevitable radicalisation of the first strategy in that 'it would be a question of putting into question again, in certain of its essential predicates, the very concept of the said ideal' (Derrida, 1994: 87). In short, this strategy is that of direct critique of capitalism. Amongst other things, such critique would involve

> the economic analysis of the market, the laws of capital, of types of capital ... liberal parliamentary democracy, modes of represen-tation and suffrage, the determining content of human rights, women's and children's rights, the current concepts of equality, liberty ... fraternity ... dignity, the relations between man and citizen. (Derrida, 1994: 87)

Much of this (if not all of it) can be recognised as constituting a familiar Marxist agenda – and although Derrida does not explicitly mention it, there is no reason why one would not add analysis of the mechanisms of exploitation to the above list. Again, whilst Derrida does not actually say as much, this second strategy could well be seen not only as the necessary complement of the first strategy, that of reformism, but its inevitable successor. To the extent that the exploitative nature of capitalism limits what can be achieved through reformist tactics, the task of the New International becomes that of direct critique, direct opposition to capitalism.

In asking how far this opposition might go in terms combating capitalism, one might think that Derrida would balk at the idea of revolution. After all, Derrida has argued in favour of excising ontol-ogising elements of Marxist thought and, traditionally, revolution has been thought of in terms of ushering in the ultimate society, communism. However, in response to an accusation of wishing to discredit the idea of revolution Derrida replied as follows:

> On more occasions than I care to count ... I have invested the word 'revolution' with a positive, affirmative value, even if the traditional figure and imageries of revolution seem to me to call for certain 'complications' .... (Sprinker, 1999: 242)

Clearly, it would be undesirable to posit revolution as a closure, as achievement of the ideal society, for we have already seen the dire results of such attempts to impose closure in reality in the form of the various failed revolutions around the world, and particularly in Eastern Europe. However, this does not discredit the option of rev-olutionary violence to overcome particular exploitative regimes where it clearly represents the course of least violence. For example, one could justify such violence to oppose a brute such as Somoza, or the racist regimes that used to dominate much of Southern Africa. However, exactly the same argument would justify violence against leftist regimes that themselves become violently exclusory, such as Mugabe's Zimbabwe, the Pol Pot regime in Cambodia, or the Chinese dictatorship, both at home, and in Tibet. In this sense the principle of least violence can be seen as more consistent than traditional leftist standpoints, which found themselves embarrassed by the practices of supposedly leftist regimes that continued with policies of repression and violence even when their tenure on power had stabilised. For Derrida, revolutionary violence would have to be aimed at moving towards the promise of democracy, at achieving a more democratic and inclusive (and therefore less violent) post-revolutionary society. It would follow that this revolutionary society itself would have to be bound by this obligation to continue to move towards the promise of democracy in order to avoid lapsing into exclusory, dictatorial practices.

This section has shown that a deconstructionist approach is eminently compatible with a de-ontologised Marxism. To the extent that Marxism is addressed to combating the exclusory nature of capitalism, its nature is to address the same injustices that deconstruction addresses. Derrida actually delineates the outlines of a political programme on the basis of Marxian influenced strategies, the first consisting of a reformist approach, whilst the second constitutes a more openly oppositional position, culminating in revolutionary violence where such an approach can be seen as the course of least violence. It is this author's contention that both of these strategies incorporate developmental moments. The first strategy, that of reformism, can clearly be seen as the point at which campaigns for greater amounts of effective development aid become essential to assist the Southern poor in their efforts not only to survive, but to improve their lives. With regard to the second strategy, development consists in the need to assist those who are violently repressed, or excluded, to resist the regime that oppresses them, so that they can take control of their lives, formulating and practising their own models of development.

4.7   CONCLUSIONS

Our analysis of deconstruction has shown that, contrary to the prejudices of many observers, it is not a relativistic discourse at all.

In fact, of the various theoretical structures we have examined, it is probably the most successful in dealing with the dilemma of foundationalism versus relativism. In formulating our theories and analytical positions we have to institute closure, this being the only access to truth that we have. However, it must always be remembered that in making a closure, we inevitably commit the violence of making exclusions, and our exclusions return to haunt us. It follows from this that the course of least violence is to try to remain open to alterity, to welcome the other.

We can also see that this approach enables us to deal more readily with difference than that of Habermas. Whereas Habermas analysed language as predisposing us to consensus because it is sustained by intersubjective understanding, Derrida problematises the relationship between language and meaning, showing that iteration constitutes alterity at the same time as it creates meaning. This means that he is not as prone to elide over difference as Habermas. Derrida's principle of the least violence also better enables us to deal with competing claims than the principle of tolerance proposed as an extension to Habermasian discourse theory. In Chapter 3 we saw that Warnke's principle of tolerance did not readily offer any key to resolving competing claims between feminists who wish to enhance the position of women and traditional cultures that wish to maintain their existing gender relations. The principle of least violence would clearly seem to indicate that where traditional mores lead to violence (e.g. female genital mutilation) they should be combated. Violence against people clearly weighs more heavily than the violation of traditions. All this need not necessarily imply a head-on confrontation between feminists and traditionalists, but a dialogue organised in line with Habermasian principles. Such a discourse would recognise that any of its decisions would be subject to revision with the minimum understanding that such decisions should reduce violence against women.

It is the point of decision that prompts the entry of politics and ethics into deconstruction. Given that we always exclude alterity in our determinations, we have a political and ethical responsibility to the other. On this basis alone it can be argued that this would constitute an ethical imperative for the North to give aid and to actively help the Southern 'other'. Post-development arguments to the effect that developmental initiatives should be condemned as invasive, or as examples of trusteeship, completely miss the point that all our dealings with the other are invasive and violent. As we have seen, none of the post-developmental programmes completely avoid the violence of exclusion, whether it be in the form of exclusion of movements that (for unspecified reasons) they do not like, such as Islamic fundamentalists, or relegation of the broad mass of people, the *min*, to political subservience to those who (by an unspecified process) are identified as the good, or the *jen*. These exclusions are all the more violent for being unexplained. The types of development that post-development observers condemn, notably top-down development that is imposed from above, are not to be condemned because they are imposed in the name of development, but because they do not seek the course of least violence. Post-development offers no solution to this problem, because, as we have just seen, it does not seek the course of least violence either with its random unexplained exclusions. By no means the least of these exclusions is the fact that there are bottom-up models of development that seek to be inclusive of the other. A central argument of this book is that we should be investigating such models of development with a view to identifying a developmental theory and practice of the least violence.

Derrida's appeal to Marxist principles illustrates how urgent it is that all concerned forces (whether Northern or Southern) should engage with development and 'Third World' issues. An ethical imperative enjoins every moral person to oppose the repressive discourse and practices of liberal capitalism. Capitalist relegation of the South to a position of economic and political subordination and exclusion must be opposed both by reformist and more radical means. This includes support for aid, as well as campaigns to make aid more inclusive so that it cannot itself be used as a vehicle for oppression. Pressure for adoption of more open consultation procedures along the lines of the ideal speech situation in all development institutions would be central to such campaigns. A central plank of any campaign of support for the South must also entail support for movements that seek liberation from exclusory, repressive regimes. In the next chapter we shall examine some examples of such movements with a view to assessing how far the critical theory of Habermas and Derrida in particular (notably the ideal speech situation and the principle of least violence) provides guidance as to which movements should be supported and what such support might involve. The chapter following that will deal with aid issues, applying the same principles to explore their implications for aid policy.

5 New Social Movements: A Subject of Development?

5.1 INTRODUCTION

In the last two chapters we have argued that the diverse projects of both Habermas and Derrida provide the elements of a new approach to development. The Habermasian ideal speech situation as modified by Blaug provides us with criteria, albeit problematic criteria, that can be used as guidelines in the attempt to maximise the fairness of discourse. A Derridian principle of least violence provides guidance as to which projects in our globalising world really are emancipatory. As such, it also provides us with a basis for identifying projects and forces that are developmental in the sense of enabling people at the grass roots to pursue their own projects and enhance their living standards. A central characteristic of developmental/emancipatory projects, movements and institutions is that they would endeavour to avoid totalisation and the exclusions that necessarily accompany it. However, this is immediately complicated by the fact that such endeavours must necessarily be unsuccessful since closure is unavoidable. Violence and exclusion cannot be completely eliminated and so we are confronted with the necessity of a calculus as to which enterprises are least exclusory and consequently most developmental – bearing in mind the inevitability of our own exclusions and the consequent need to try and minimise them. Despite these inherent difficulties in the principle of least violence this chapter will argue that it provides us with an effective means of differentiating between that which is more developmental/emancipatory and that which is less so. Certainly, we shall demonstrate that it is more effective than the explanations offered by post-development theorists.

A central theme in much post-development analysis concerns the leading role of new social movements (NSMs) in achieving various emancipatory projects. Usually this role is predicated on an attribution of authenticity to such movements. They are seen as authentic products of grass-roots activism charged with the task of preserving and protecting the traditional societies and cultures of the social majorities, particularly from the predations of neo-liberal forces. However, it should be clear by now that such assertions of authenticity can themselves be deconstructed. As we saw in Chapter 2, Esteva and Prakash make an assumption of pristine originarity and associated virtue about Triqui society that masks apparent relations of gender inequality. Similarly, Rahnema resorted to a reductive account of origins in his characterisation of vernacular societies as untouched by any aspect of capitalism prior to their infection by *homo oeconomicus*. This was despite plentiful evidence of high levels of trade in various areas of the world prior to the emergence of *homo oeconomicus* dated by Rahnema in the seventeenth century.

The projects that post-development analysts attribute to the new social movements are also marked by closure, none more clearly than that of Rahnema with his vision of an authentic society based on Confucian principles in which the *min* (the mediocre majority) are ruled by the *jen* (the minority of the truly deserving and good). However, such closure is also (at least implicitly) apparent in the work of Esteva and Prakash when they reject modern education and medicine, a decision suggesting, amongst other things, that traditional societies should be left prey to diseases that can only be cured by modern medicines.

All this is suggestive that authenticity is a far from satisfactory criterion for gauging the emancipatory credentials of a NSM. Indeed, the post-development theorists themselves implicitly recognise this by excluding certain movements from what Esteva and Prakash termed the 'epic unfolding at the grass roots'. Such exclusions are made irrespective of any claims to authenticity made by these movements. Notably, fundamentalists of any stripe are defined as non-emancipatory, a decision that does not fit comfortably with a criterion of authenticity given that the central claim of most fundamentalists pertains to their authenticity. As we have seen, the post-development analysts seem unable to provide an explanation of why such movements should be blacklisted.

If authenticity represents a problematic ground for support of NSMs it might be argued that firmer ground could be found in the analysis of those commentators who first identified such movements as a force for progress. NSMs were first identified in the industrial states in the form of organisations such as the peace and women's movements. They have often been seen as a post-industrial/post-communist phenomenon. This line of thought sees the transition to post-industrial society and concomitant working-class fragmentation as having led to the decline of class politics as manifested in the old class-based parties. Social fragmentation and differentiation have led to the emergence of non-class-based identities such as gender and ethnicity, which form the basis for NSMs pursuing social agendas such as gender equity and arms control (Johnston *et al.* in Larana *et al.*, 1994: 6–8). Schuurman summarises this analysis as follows:

> The new line adopted was that new social movements were associations within the subaltern classes where (embryonic) processes took place concerning the creation of new, non-commoditive values, new lines of horizontal communication – in short the creation of a new identity (Evers 1985), an identity, contrary to the universality of the modernity projects, with its own localised goals of emancipation, which did not lead to a bid for political power, but was based in local movements with multiple identities located in civil society, stressing new ways of social communication (solidarity and mutual understanding) and a new harmonic relationship with nature. (Schuurman, 1993: 189)

Thus, the old mass movements pursuing universal goals such as the emancipation of the proletariat are seen as having been superseded by local movements with more limited aims that generally do not include seizing political power. Flacks also argues that mass parties have tended to become redundant partly because they failed to properly represent minorities (e.g. women, ethnic minorities) in their effort to represent the majority of their membership (Flacks in Larana *et al.*, 1994: 336).

Melucci focuses on changes in the power structure reducing the role of the state. He argues that state power has been eroded at the international level by the development of 'a tightly interdependent system of transnational relationships', while it has been 'subdivided ... from below' by a proliferation of sub-national governmental authorities, 'and by an ensemble of interwoven organizations which combine inextricably the public and the private' (Melucci, 1992: 70). This has led to the growth of a number of unaccountable power centres. Social movements arise out of popular attempts to exert some control and make demands on these power centres (1992: 71). They challenge the power of such centres to produce information, or knowledge. Melucci elaborates this point, noting that this challenge prevents the channels of representation and decision-making in pluralist societies from adopting instrumental rationality as the only logic with which to govern complexity. Such rationality applies solely to procedures, and imposes the criterion of efficiency and effectiveness as the only measure of sense. The action of movements reveals that the neutral rationality of means masks interest and forms of power. (Melucci, 1992: 75)

According to this view NSMs come into being as a result of attempts by people at the grass roots to exert control over unaccountable power centres that have been created as part of the process of globalisation. By way of example one might cite the activities of various groups, notably the organisations that campaigned unceasingly to make the World Bank take greater account of the frequently disastrous social effects of its neo-liberal conditionality. They eventually succeeded in forcing the Bank to open a dialogue in the form of the Structural Adjustment Participatory Review International Network (SAPRIN), which involves the Bank, various civil society organisations and governments in an initiative to investigate the effects of adjustment and recommend changes in Bank conditionality (see http://www.saprin.org).

While the activities of such forces as the women's movement, gay rights groups, or cultural organisations may not take the form of a traditional political discourse, Alvarez *et al.* insist that they are nevertheless political. They base this conclusion on the definition of cultural politics given by Jordan and Weedon:

The legitimation of social relations of inequality, and the struggle to transform them, are central concerns of CULTURAL POLITICS. Cultural politics fundamentally determine the meanings of social practices, and, moreover, which groups and individuals have the power to define these meanings. Cultural politics are also concerned with subjectivity and identity, since culture plays a central role in constituting our sense of ourselves ... The forms of subjectivity that we inhabit play a crucial part in determining whether we accept or contest existing power relations. Moreover, for marginalized and oppressed groups, the construction of new and resistant identities is a key dimension of a wider political struggle to transform society. (Alvarez *et al.*, 1998: 5–6)

NSMs may thus be identified as central protagonists in cultural politics, both as forces in struggle against social inequalities, and as focuses for construction of identities of resistance. This is borne out by the views of Dagnino 'that cultural contestations are not mere "by-products" of political struggle but are instead constitutive of the efforts of social movements to redefine the meaning and the limits of the political system itself' (1998: 7). By struggling for marginalised cultures and groups NSMs seek to deconstruct the dominant culture as defined by the power centres, and to reinstate excluded cultures and interests so that they can have a voice in the ongoing definition of society and the political system.

Whereas analysts like Johnston and Melucci focus on phenomena such as the decline of class politics and the state (both of which could be seen as functions of globalisation) in creating the conditions for the rise of NSMs, Dagnino uses Gramscian theory to develop an emancipatory discourse based around social movements. She argues as follows:

> There is widespread recognition that the theory of hegemony implies a rupture with the notion that 'preconstituted' political subjects are deduced from positions within the economic production process through class reductionism ... The hegemonic construction requires 'the attainment of a "cultural–social" unity through which a multiplicity of dispersed wills, with heterogeneous aims, are welded together with a single aim, on the basis of an equal and common perception of the world' (Gramsci, 1971: 349). As a process of articulation of the different interests necessary to build a 'collective will' and achieve active consent, hegemony is itself a process of constitution of subjects. Such a process takes place on a ground that is not strictly defined by economic structural forces but by a broader process of moral and intellectual reform ... Thus, the capacity to transcend particular, corporative interests, to compromise and negotiate, are crucial hegemonic features insofar [as] they make possible this articulation of different interests ... The 'single aim' and the 'equal and common conception of the world' are not points of departure ensured by predefined subjects and contents but a processual construction, an articulation always submitted to reelaboration and renewal, conceived as the basis for collective political action toward social transformation. Moreover, this conception of hegemony as articulation opens the door for a consideration of

basic subjects and the process of building their own collective identities. The collective elaboration of the basis for such an articulation embodies the core of and the greatest challenge to hegemonic construction. (Dagnino, 1998: 42)

In other words, Dagnino argues that a Gramscian perspective dispenses with the idea of economic class as determining politics in such a way that all workers have common and coincident interests. Its incorporation of a cultural moment leads to a perception of cultural differences and awareness of a variety of oppressed groups that have their own aims and projects. Dagnino uses the concept of hegemonic construction to argue that building a hegemony of the oppressed requires welding such groups together on a basis of consent. Hence the need for compromise and negotiation to achieve unity, an 'articulation of different interests' with a single emancipatory aim. Moreover, the process of negotiation is ongoing, so that individual groups (subjects) do not lose their autonomy and become subsumed in the compelling necessity to achieve the single aim. In this way Dagnino explicates a possibility for developing an emancipatory project on the basis of a continually negotiated alliance of variant forces of the excluded. As Dagnino puts it:

Gramsci's ... emphasis on the primacy of politics understood as an ethical-cultural process, constituted an integrative basis from which it was possible to address the emerging social movements as well as the multiplicity of concerns and interests these movements brought to the political scene. For their bearers, such a view expresses a number of motivations: among them an urge to break from class reductionism without falling into liberal pluralism and a need to account for difference without forsaking the historical concern of the Left with equality. (1998: 42)

This account of an NSM-based strategy embraces the following elements: first, a commitment to address the multiple projects of different oppressed groups: secondly, a consistently radical edge that prevents its comprehension of difference from being subsumed into the liberal view of democracy as a competition for influence between roughly equal interest groups: and thirdly, the commitment to a collective emancipation of variant groups that is nevertheless compatible with the traditional Leftist (and also developmental) goal of achieving a fair and egalitarian society.

It can be seen that Dagnino's use of Gramscian concepts enables her to develop a vision of an emancipatory project based around social movements, a vision that is decidedly reminiscent of Derrida's New International. Furthermore, it can be seen as a movement in the broad direction of the Habermasian and Derridian principles that we are advocating as a basis for development thinking. The focus on building an articulation of social movements based on negotiation and compromise, and to account for difference without sacrificing Leftist egalitarian principles, are all redolent of the principles of Habermasian discourse theory with its requirements that all parties receive a fair hearing. Furthermore her assertion that any articulation of such movements must take place on the basis of continued re-elaboration and renewal adheres to the sense of the principle of least violence in its avoidance of any absolute closure.

Flacks takes a similar line to Dagnino, arguing that 'if the Left is understood as a cumulative struggle for the democratization of society, then social movements ... are the real embodiment of the Left tradition' (Flacks in Larana *et al.*, 1994: 338–9). He throws a little more light on how a coalition between NSMs might be achieved, suggesting that

> 'common ground' as articulated by contemporary movement theorists does not require that discrete movements abandon their separate cultures and claims. Instead, what can be imagined are efforts to find programmatic ways to respond to the shared needs of movement constitutencies. (Flacks, 1994: 346)

To illustrate his point Flacks observes that in the USA, socialisation of medicine would serve the interests of a variety of interests, including workers, the gay community as it tries to cope with AIDS, and poor ethnic groups. One does not have to search too far to find such common ground in the South, most notably in the opposition of numerous groups to the neo-liberal development policy of Structural Adjustment, which has wrought havoc in many poor countries.

All of this argumentation indicates how NSMs can serve as an emancipatory force, broadly in accordance with Habermasian and Derridian principles. As yet it has not afforded us any explanation or criteria as to why some groups might be deemed emancipatory and others not. In the next section we shall examine some specific movements with a view to establishing whether or not Habermasian discourse theory and deconstruction can throw some light on this issue.

5.2 SOCIAL MOVEMENTS AND PERMANENT REVOLUTION

When analysts examine how far NSMs can play a revolutionary role, especially in the South, they often focus on the Zapatistas of Mexico. It will be remembered that Esteva and Prakash identify them as the very model of a post-developmental organisation. As we shall see, there are good reasons for seeing the Zapatitas as a model for NSM activity.

The Zapatista Army of National Liberation (EZLN) first made an impact on the world stage on 1 January 1994 when they occupied the city of San Cristobal de las Casas and six other towns in an action that was timed to coincide with the entry into force of the North American Free Trade Agreement (NAFTA). The people of the Chiapas region, who form the backbone of the Zapatistas, have traditionally been marginalised, receiving little in the way of infrastructure from the government. Educational facilities are so sparse that over half the population of the area are illiterate, whilst the inadequacy of health provision is reflected in statistics like the infant mortality rate, which stood at 51.7 deaths per 100,000 in Chiapas, compared with 34.8 for the country as a whole in the early 1990s (Cecena and Barreda in Holloway and Pelaez, 1998: 52–4). In addition, local people had been more and more marginalised by the demands of cattle ranchers and then oil companies for their land. In the words of Holloway and Pelaez, 'by the beginning of 1994, they were facing extermination as a community' (1998: 1). NAFTA, with its threat of cheap food imports that would undercut their own produce, came as a final blow that prompted the uprising of 1994.

However, observers of both left and right were soon to realise that this was not a traditional rebellion, but something quite new. The Zapatistas represented a departure from the norm in several respects, most notably the following. Firstly, the Zapatistas reject any suggestion of taking power, either in their own right, or as part of the existing apparatus of government. One of their communiqués explained this as follows:

> The 'centre' asks us, demands of us, that we should sign a peace agreement quickly and convert ourselves into an 'institutional' political force, that is to say, convert ourselves into yet another part of the machinery of power. To them we answer 'NO' and they

do not understand it ... They do not understand that we do not want offices or posts in the government. They do not understand that we are struggling not for the stairs to be swept clean from the top to the bottom, but for there to be no stairs, for there to be no kingdom at all. (Holloway and Pelaez, 1998: 4)

The traditional leftist aim of gaining political power in order to impose a revolutionary agenda is dispensed with, a policy that effectively curtails opportunities and temptations for leadership figures to sell out to the Mexican state.

Secondly, the Zapatistas have not essentialised their identity in terms of limiting their membership to any particular grouping. Although the majority of their membership consists of people from the ethnic groups indigenous to the Chiapas region, they do not identify themselves as representing any particular group, or area, taking as a slogan: 'For Humanity against Neoliberalism'. An oft-quoted passage from one of Subcomandante Marcos' communiqués expresses this as follows:

Marcos is gay in San Francisco, a black in South Africa, Asian in Europe, a Chicano in San Isidro, an anarchist in Spain, a Palestinian in Israel, an indigenous person in the streets of San Cristobal, a gang member in Neza, a rocker on campus, a Jew in Germany, an ombudsman in the Department of Defence, a feminist in a political party, a communist in the post-Cold War period, a prisoner in Cintalapa, a pacifist in Bosnia, a Mapuche in the Andes, a teacher in the National Confederation of Educational Workers, an artist without a gallery or a portfolio, a housewife in any neighbourhood in any city in any part of Mexico on a Saturday night, a guerrilla in Mexico at the end of the twentieth century, a striker in the CTM, a sexist in the feminist movement, a woman alone in a Metro station at 10 p.m., a retired person standing around in the Zocalo, a peasant without land, an underground editor, an unemployed worker, a doctor with no office, a non-conformist student, a dissident against neoliberalism, a writer without books or readers, and a Zapatista in the Mexican southeast. In other words, Marcos is a human being in this world. Marcos is every untolerated, oppressed, exploited minority that is resisting and saying 'Enough'! (Holloway and Pelaez, 1998: 10–11).

In this way the Zapatistas avoid any closure in the form of a defined membership which excludes those who do not fit the definition. They claim unity with 'all those "without face, without voice, without future" who stand against neoliberalism' (Holloway and Pelaez, 1998: 11).

This inclusive position involves active efforts to incorporate women into every level of the movement, most notably through the Revolutionary Women's Law, which the Zapatistas published in 1994 on the same day as their uprising, and in the same publication as their First Declaration of the Lacandon Jungle, Today We Say 'Enough!'. The law guarantees women's rights to education, health care, employment with fair wages, to decide who they marry and to limit the number of their children, and their right to be protected by law from physical attack and rape. The following articles are particularly worth noting:

> Article Four: Women have the right to participate in community affairs and hold posts if they are freely and democratically elected ...
> Article Nine: Women may hold leadership posts in the organization and military rank in the revolutionary armed forces.
> Article Ten: Women will enjoy all rights and obligations established in revolutionary laws and regulations. (Millan, in Holloway and Pelaez, 1998: 74–5)

The above articles ensure that women have the right to be heard, to hold office, to participate in any decisions that affect them, and to be treated equally by revolutionary laws. This comes very close to meeting Habermas' ideal speech situation, at least as far as women are concerned. They cannot be silenced, intimidated, or excluded, and it could be argued that the rights to hold office and to be treated equally under the law guarantee them the assurance that this position cannot be eroded. The latter point effectively means that Blaug's Principle of Preservation (P) is observed by the Zapatistas. This principle stipulated that to be legitimate the outcome of discourse must not damage the ideal speech situation. Thus, the Women's Revolutionary Law prevents the Zapatistas from retreating from their commitment to the equal treatment of women.

It might be suggested that the mere commitment of a law to paper means nothing in itself, and there are all too many examples of supposedly emancipatory regimes passing laws that they then subverted, or simply failed to apply. However, Millan and other observers contend that the Zapatistas actually do apply their laws in a consistent manner. Moreover, principles remarkably similar to those prescribed under the ideal speech situation are central to the organisation of the Zapatistas. The central concept underlying the organisation is known as *mandar obedeciendo* (to command obeying). This principle of command obeying comes out of the customs of local peasant communities where all important discussions are debated by the whole community until consensus is reached and leaders can be recalled if their performance is unsatisfactory (see Lorenzano, 1998: 129–30 and Holloway, 1998: 164 in Holloway and Pelaez, 1998). As practised by the Zapatistas it essentially entails direct democracy and revocability of office (in Holloway and Pelaez, 1998: 129–130). Lorenzano points out that this sounds similar to previous attempts at revolutionary organisation such as the Paris Commune, or the Russian soviets. However, the Zapatistas are different from the latter examples in that they do not restrict democratic practices to a minority, or vanguard group. The whole of the Zapatista's membership base is involved in their decision-making process. Holloway comments on this as follows:

> ... the decision to go to war was not taken by some central committee and then handed down, but was discussed by all the communities in village assemblies. The whole organization is structured along the same principle: the ruling body, the CCRI, is composed of recallable delegates chosen by the different ethnic groups (Tzotzil, Tzeltal, Tojolabal and Chol), and each ethnic group in each region has its own committees chosen in assemblies on the same principle. (1998: 165)

This obviously means that the decision-making process takes time, but it has the benefit of involving all of the Zapatista support base in decisions, thus opening democratic participation to all. The principle of revocability also radicalises democracy to the extent that it reduces the likelihood that elected officials will abuse their positions or renege on promises they made in order to be elected. Holloway argues that 'a deepening of democracy through "all kinds of participation"' is at the heart of the Zapatista project (1998: 155). Again, the measures to ensure that everybody is heard, and that leadership figures and groups cannot acquire more power than other participants in the decision-making process, are all indicative that the Zapatistas come very close to meeting the criteria for the ideal speech situation.

It follows from this that the Zapatistas do not have any rigid programme that envisages some final end state such as communism. The fact that decisions and policy are decided collectively means that there cannot be a pre-decided programme for the movement, since any policy proposal must receive popular approval. This does not mean that the Zapatistas have no goals that they want to achieve for their membership. For example, a central aim of their dialogues with the Mexican Government consists in winning and defining indigenous rights. However, this is not an end goal, but a basis for moving on to other issues of importance to the oppressed. This lack of a set policy agenda for Zapatista praxis is a large part of the reason why they have no ambition to seize the state, or to become a government party. The announcement of such a goal would effectively set a limit on their emancipatory project. It would be a signal to the Mexican Government that the movement could be brought under control in exchange for political concessions, perhaps the chance to have a role in governance and claim a share of the spoils. Indeed, the efforts of the Mexican state negotiators have been directed to the aim of defining and institutionalising the Zapatistas, precisely with the intention of limiting them. To the extent that the state can classify them as a local political party, or a civil rights group, it can limit their influence, claiming that the EZLN's proper area of activity is limited to the Chiapas area or to the concerns of indigenous people. Any such outcome would be the beginning of a process through which the government would limit and circumscribe the emancipatory enterprise that the Zapatistas have set in motion. For their part the Zapatistas have stubbornly refused such classification. Holloway summarises the situation as follows:

> The struggle of the state against the Zapatistas since the declaration of the cease-fire has been a struggle to define, to classify, to limit; the struggle of the Zapatistas against the state has been the struggle to break out, to break the barriers, to overflow, to refuse definition or to accept and transcend definition. (Holloway, 1998: 172)

In this way, the Zapatistas have refused to institute any form of closure on their project, or to accept any kind of closure being imposed on it. Theirs is a permanent revolution in the sense that it has no horizon. This is very much in line with the policy of avoiding adoption of an essentialised and closed identity. The Zapatista enterprise is defined as open to all of the oppressed and their projects for emancipation, though there is a particular focus on those opposing neo-liberalism. They are markedly close to fulfilling deconstructionist criteria of least violence.

It is worth observing that the Zapatistas have excellent credentials with regard to authenticity. Their democratic practice of command obeying is drawn from local custom and they are clearly a grass-roots movement that empowers the grass roots rather than a few representatives. This quality motivates Esteva and Prakash to focus particularly on the EZLN as an exemplary emancipatory movement. However, it is worth noting that the movement will work in opposition to customary practices that are unjust, as with the Women's Revolutionary Law, which seeks to transform the traditionally subordinate role of women. Clearly, authenticity is not the bottom line in assessing the emancipatory credentials of the Zapatistas. It may be argued that their campaign is primarily concerned with the overthrow, or radical reform (through largely non-violent tactics), of a violently oppressive system in the attempt to found an inclusive radically democratic system so that the various peoples of Mexico can pursue their own projects. In this sense it is more about what might be termed a 'development of least violence'.

Most NSMs have a more contradictory profile than the Zapatistas, incorporating elements of closure and exclusion along with some emancipatory aspects. Such an example is the Coalition of Workers, Peasants, and Students of the Isthmus (COCEI) of Juchitan in Southern Mexico, which was the subject of an informative case study by Jeffrey Rubin. COCEI operated through 15 years of repression, helping Jucheticos to gain 'the rights to speak out in agrarian agencies and labor courts, solve local problems by local means, use their own language in official proceedings, gain access to complex networks of information, and maintain their own ritual practices' (Rubin in Alvarez *et al.*, 1998: 150), as well as some protection for small-scale agriculture (1998: 142). They even succeeded in being elected to govern the city in 1989. Rubin argues that while COCEI displays some of the characteristics that NSM theorists praise, these are mixed with 'other, less obviously praiseworthy attributes'. Thus, the COCEI leadership is responsive to many grass-roots demands and needs, and women are actively involved in the work of the organisation, all characteristics that can be seen as progressive. However, it is also exclusory, maintaining a hostile stance to other leftist parties and to outsiders, almost to the point of violence (Rubin in Alvarez *et al.*, 1998: 148). While women play a significant role in social mobilisation for COCEI, they are excluded from leadership positions, and the organisation has not done anything to combat gender roles through which women are exploited (Rubin in Alvarez *et al.*, 1998: 157–8). Moreover, COCEI was lacking in internal democracy with its leadership regarding themselves as a Leninist vanguard group. In short, COCEI displays significant exclusory and violent characteristics.

Rubin argues that these contradictory aspects of COCEI were integral to its success. The movement's 'flexible and changing mixtures of Leninist and new social-movement political practices' enabled it to use a mixture of discourses to good effect and to open up multiple spaces for popular complaint and activism. For example, COCEI's official discourse of Leninism was effective in formal political contexts, whilst the popular discourse shaped by the women activists was effective in mobilising support at the grass roots and in giving form to popular grievances that fuelled many of the movement's campaigns (Rubin in Alvarez *et al.*, 1998: 160–1).

At this point we might consider whether or not COCEI would be classified as part of the post-development emancipatory trend. Post-development theorists would presumably be somewhat averse to the movement's endorsement of Leninism, a Western meta-discourse that owes little if anything to the Mexican context. One might hope that its lack of internal democracy, exclusivism, and sexism would also militate against COCEI's classification as an emancipatory movement. However, we have already seen that various post-development analysts lapse into similarly violent exclusions where these are deemed to be authentic elements of grass-roots culture. It is worth noting that Escobar (in a jointly authored piece) approvingly notes how the women of COCEI have constructed a grass-roots discourse of resistance (Escobar with Alvarez and Dagnino, 1998: 19). Indeed, the fact that this discourse coexists with the official Leninist discourse is indicative of an element of openness in COCEI's ideological orientation, albeit problematic. One must also pay attention to the fact that COCEI has delivered substantive benefits to Jucheticos at the grass roots, a factor that suggests they are succeeding in achieving some level of development for local people.

All this is indicative of a complicated calculus in any judgement of whether or not a movement can be considered emancipatory whatever criteria are used in making the decision. It also indicates

that authenticity is a somewhat less reliable indicator of the emancipatory nature of a movement than the criteria we have advocated
in previous chapters, those pertaining to the ideal speech situation
and the principle of least violence. The EZLN's popular roots are
undoubtedly a key to its continued vitality in Mexico and Chiapas,
but as we have already noted, its untiring internal battle against
gender inequality and its determination to support the oppressed in
general are surely more reliable indicators of a genuinely emancipatory stance. COCEI can be seen to combine emancipatory and
repressive features, but in such a way as to bring about certain gains
for the grass roots. It might be expected that many movements will
fall into this category, combining exclusory deformations with a
genuinely emancipatory moment that ethically demands support.
This should not be too surprising. We have already seen that any
statement, any establishment of an institution or movement, entails
some sort of closure with its attendant exclusions and violence. The
key is to minimise such exclusion and violence. Such criteria enable
us to differentiate between the Zapatistas, who eschew the violence
of definition, and COCEI, which practises certain exclusions.
Further, they enable us to differentiate between the Zapatistas and
COCEI on the one hand, and fascist movements on the other. The
former conceive emancipation in terms of empowerment of those
who are currently oppressed by the violence of the system so that
they can have a voice in decisions that affect their lives. Fascism on
the other hand envisages a centralisation of power, and to the extent
that there is an emancipatory vision it is premised on explicit
violence towards others who are identified as national, or ethnic
enemies. While this does not suggest unquestioning acceptance of
COCEI's violence, it does indicate an emancipatory moment that is
absent in fascism, which is based on systematic violence and
exclusion. In this way the criteria pertaining to the ideal speech
situation and the principle of least violence lead to a more reliable
reading of whether or not a NSM is emancipatory than those
espoused by the post-development analysts.

It will be remembered that Esteva and Prakash excluded Islamic
fundamentalists from their grass-roots epic without bothering to
explain why. Islamists were placed in the same category of fascists,
seemingly on the assumption that their reprehensible nature was
self-evident. Why? We have already seen that several of the post-
developmentalists essentialise supposedly authentic grass-roots
movements, eliding over various types of exclusion. It seems

reasonable to speculate that they have similarly essentialised Islam, but to the detriment of Muslim movements in this instance, focusing on the exclusory violence and terrorism that is popularly associated with Islamic fundamentalism, especially since the atrocities committed in Washington DC and New York on 11 September 2001. But how accurate is it to generalise about Islamism on the basis of such openly violent and repressive movements as the Taliban and the al-Quaida group? In the next section we shall examine some trends in Islamic thought and popular organisation in order to see if the criteria we have derived from the work of Habermas and Derrida can throw any light on this question.

5.3   AN ISLAMIC POLITICS OF LEAST VIOLENCE?

Islamic fundamentalism, or Islamism, conceived as the project of founding an Islamic state based on *shari'a* law, is generally characterised as anti-democratic and repressive of non-Muslims and women in general. A fairly typical example is provided by Sidahmed and Ehteshami in the Introduction to their reader, *Islamic Fundamentalism*, wherein they state that 'Islamists adhere with varying degrees of emphasis to the supremacy of *shari'a*.' Since Islamist leaders have appropriated the right to specify what is in accordance with *shari'a* and what is not, they are 'denying everyone else a similar share in public affairs ... It follows, therefore, that the Islamist ideology and the ideology of democracy are inherently incompatible' (Sidahmed and Ehteshami, 1996: 14). Undoubtedly, many Islamist movements actually are founded on such views, not least the Taliban and those taking their lead from Osama bin Laden. However, an examination of the variety of trends within Islamist thought reveals some significant departures from this characterisation.

Robert Lee focuses on Mohammed Arkoun, who starts from a position of acknowledging that *shari'a* was developed over a period of centuries by a variety of authorities who must have been sociologically influenced by the societies that they lived in. To the extent that their contributions to *shari'a* are shaped by their respective backgrounds, this detracts from claims that *shari'a* is of universal relevance to all societies at all times. Flesh and blood human beings mediate the truth and so all the influences acting on the interpreters of Islam must be taken into account in weighing their pronouncements. Two things follow from this point for Arkoun. Firstly, the claims of particular tendencies and movements within Islam to a monopoly on the truth are erroneous and reductive of the truth of

Islam. Thus, he condemns the Muslim Brotherhood and revolutionary Islamist movements for falsely laying claim to being the only genuine representatives of Islam and for being reductionist of Islamic truth (Lee, 1997: 156). Secondly, Arkoun maintains that an understanding of Islamic truth can only be achieved by a considered, scientific examination of all the trends within Islam (1994: 153).

Lee intimates that Arkoun may put a little too much faith in social science. Arkoun argues that social science must articulate the multiplicity of Islamic discourses by means of its own constantly revised discourses and methods. Lee points out that if science is constantly changing its discourses, criteria and methods, how can we know that it is progressing and that its analysis of Islam will get nearer to the truth (1997: 163–4)? This raises the question of the relativism of discourses in a way that is reminiscent of Foucault, which is suggestive of a position that each discourse is equally (in)valid, or that each trend within Islam has an equal claim to (un)truth. It may be argued that Arkoun is able to avoid this blind alley with his injunction that the examination of all the trends in Islam must take account of what is unthought. Lee explains that he means by this 'that which is unthinkable (e.g. atheism); that which is beyond the limits of scientific thought, hence not yet thought; that which is masked or hidden; that which is rejected in the course of scientific development; and that which is simply forgotten' (Lee, 1997: 158). This is clearly analogous to Derrida's conception of the promise, or the excess of our formulations. If we adhere to this view, Arkoun's project becomes one of steady progress and increased understanding of Islamic truth as one examines its various manifestations, but one that can never end because of the need to account for the interpretation to come.

Clearly Arkoun's approach is very different from that of such organisations as the Muslim Brotherhood, or the Islamic state of Iran. In pointing out that *shari'a* and other Muslim texts are the result of the mediations of interpreters, such as the *ulema*, and that they are marked by the sociological conditions of this mediation, Arkoun opens up the exclusivist elements of *shari'a* for reconsideration and revision. Thus, those elements of *shari'a* currently thought to discriminate against women and non-Muslims could be reformed.

Abdullahi An-Naim follows a similar line to that of Arkoun. An-Naim starts from the position that Muslims consider *shari'a* to be divine, but that *shari'a* is unequal in its effects on particular groups, notably non-Muslims and women. For example, Muslim women are excluded from any public office that involves giving them authority over men. This element of *shari'a* is based on verse 4:34 of the *Qur'an*, which states that men are the guardians of women (An-Naim, 1990: 87–8). Non-Muslims are the subject of discrimination in that they are subject to the *jizya* poll tax. It is sometimes claimed that this is not discriminatory in that they are not liable to pay the *zakat* tax levied on Muslims. However, this does not take into account the fact that 'Jizya was intended, by the terms of the Qur'an itself, to signify submission and humiliation of the non-Muslims who had to pay it' (An-Naim, 1990: 89). Moreover, the testimony of women and non-believers is inadmissible in serious criminal cases (1990: 90). An-Naim identifies a variety of other instances in which *shari'a* is discriminatory (1990: 176).

However, even amongst those groups and scholars who believe in the divinity of *shari'a* and the need to apply it exactly, there are differences of opinion as to how it should be applied. An-Naim notes that

> [w]hereas the Absolutists (extreme proponents of the shari'a state) and Mawdudi see the whole of Shari'a and jurisprudence as directly applicable, Asad, Perwez, Hakim, and Javid Iqbal speak of the Qur'an and Sunna as the basis of the law with room for contemporary human discretion in its interpretation and application. (1990: 38)

Such variations demonstrate that even amongst the most orthodox of fundamentalist Muslims there are questions as to how *shari'a* should be applied.

An-Naim moves on from this basis to show how the principle of *ijtihad* played a significant role in the formation of *shari'a*. He defines this principle as follows:

> Ijtihad literally means hard striving or strenuousness, but technically it means exercising independent juristic reasoning to provide answers when the Qur'an and Sunna are silent. Sunna is reported in support of ijtihad as a source of Shari'a ... the exercise of ijtihad ... is relevant to the interpretation of the Qur'an and Sunna. Whenever a principle or rule of Shari'a is based on the general meaning or broad implications of a text of Qur'an or Sunna, as opposed to the direct ruling of a clear and definite text, the link between the text and the principle or rule of Shari'a is established

through juristic reasoning. It is hard to imagine any text of the Qur'an or Sunna, however clear and definite it may appear to be, that does not need this type of ijtihad for its interpretation and application in concrete situations. (An-Naim, 1990: 27)

Ijtihad was used quite extensively in the formulation of *shari'a* in the eighth and ninth centuries until the point that *shari'a* constituted a mature legal system at which time it fell into disuse and the gates of *ijtihad* were closed. An-Naim notes that it has been suggested that *ijtihad* could be used in the present day to reform *shari'a* law. He observes that such prospects are limited by the fact that *ijtihad* is limited to 'matters not governed by clear and definite texts of Qur'an or Sunna' (An-Naim, 1990: 28). However, a precedent to suggest that this limit need not apply 'can be found in the fact that Umar, the second caliph and one of the leading companions, had exercised ijtihad in matters that were actually governed by clear and definite texts of Qur'an and Sunna' (1990: 28). An-Naim provides two examples where Umar took such action. First, he abandoned the practice of paying a portion of state funds to those whose allegiance to the Muslims had to be secured with material incentives. Umar explained his action by saying that the practice had been started when the Muslims were weak and needed allies, but that this was no longer the case and so there was no reason to continue with it. Secondly, he refused to distribute captured lands to Muslim soldiers, arguing that such resources were needed by the Muslim state to maintain its armies. Both of these practices had been specified in the Qur'an, but Umar abandoned them for policy reasons in accordance with his view of what was best for the Muslim community. An-Naim argues that the precedent of Umar indicates that 'policy considerations may justify applying a rule derived through ijtihad even if that required overriding clear and definite texts of the Qur'an and Sunna' (1990: 28). He concludes that 'contemporary Muslims have the competence to ... exercise ijtihad even in matters governed by clear and definite texts of the Qur'an and Sunna as long as the outcome of such ijtihad is consistent with the essential message of Islam' (1990: 28–9).

An-Naim moves on to develop his argument as to how *shari'a*'s exclusivist provisions might be reformed. The Qur'an is a central basis of *shari'a*, but An-Naim notes that some verses of the Qur'an and Sunna are inconsistent with each other. He observes that whereas the earlier Qur'an of the Meccan stage instructs the Prophet and his followers to practice peaceful persuasion and allow others freedom of choice in accepting or rejecting Islam, the Qur'an and Sunna of the Medina stage clearly sanctioned, and even required under certain conditions, the use of force to compel the unbelievers either to embrace Islam or to suffer one of the options provided for under Shari'a, which included death, enslavement, or some other unpleasant consequence. (An-Naim, 1990: 49)

The founding jurists of Islam used a process known as *naskh* (abrogation or repeal) to solve these inconsistencies by arguing that the later Medinan verses repealed the earlier Meccan verses. Thus, the verses enjoining a militant and forceful Islam became the basis for *shari'a*. An-Naim argues that 'since the technique of naskh has been employed in the past to develop Shari'a which has hitherto been accepted as the authentic and genuine Islamic model, the same technique may be employed today to produce an authentic and genuine modern Islamic law' (1990: 49).

A rationale for repealing the Medinan verses in favour of the Meccan verses is provided by reference to the thought of Mahmoud Mohammed Taha. Taha argued that the Meccan verses are more fundamental inasmuch as they present the eternal message of Islam 'emphasizing the inherent dignity of all human beings, regardless of gender, religious belief, race, and so forth' (An-Naim, 1990: 52). These verses recognise the equality of men and women and propound a message based on freedom of choice and non-compulsion. Only when this approach was violently rejected by the society of the day did the message of the Meccan verses give way to the Medinan message, which provided a basis for the survival of Islam in the context of the seventh century. For Taha, the Medinan verses were a response to the conditions of the time, whilst the Meccan verses gave the first and essential message of Islam. The founding jurists used *naskh* to replace this message with the Medinan verses which were appropriate to that stage of Islam. However, there is no reason why that use of *naskh* should be permanent. Indeed, Taha would argue that such a contention makes no sense, for if the Medinan message were to remain permanent what would be the point of having revealed the Meccan message? It follows that the Meccan message was revealed first because it is more fundamental to Islam, whilst the Medinan verses were a response to contingent events. An-Naim summarises the culminating logic of Taha's analysis as follows:

> Ustadh Mahmoud proposed the evolution of the basis of Islamic law from the texts of the Medina stage to that of the earlier Mecca period. In other words, the evolutionary principle of interpretation is nothing more than reversing the process of naskh or abrogation so that those texts which were abrogated in the past can be enacted into law now, with the consequent abrogation of texts that used to be enacted as Shari'a. Verses that used to be enacted as Shari'a shall be repealed, and verses that used to be repealed shall be enacted as modern Islamic law. Since this proposal would found modern principles of public law on one class of Qur'an and Sunna texts as opposed to another class of those texts, the resultant body of law would be as Islamic as Shari'a has been ... a system of public law based on the Qur'an and Sunna, albeit 'not necessarily the classical medieval Shari'a,' would be the modern 'Shari'a'. (An-Naim, 1990: 56)

In this way, An-Naim follows Taha in elaborating a basis for a thoroughgoing reform of *shari'a* resulting in a legal code based on the Meccan verses of the Qur'an enshrining principles of gender, religious, and racial equality.

The significance of this example is that An-Naim's proposal falls within the precepts of Islamism in that it can be taken as envisaging the establishment of an Islamic state with the application of *shari'a* law, albeit reformed through the application of *naskh* as envisaged by Taha. Consequently, it shows that Islam, even a fundamentalist Islam (if one agrees that the Islamic state and *shari'a* are the markers of fundamentalist Islam) need not be exclusivist and repressive.

These intellectual trends are also being manifested in the projects of some NSMs in certain parts of the Islamic world. Raymond Baker identifies the emergence of what he terms a 'centrist' tendency, or Islamic *Wasittiyah* in Egypt. He does not focus on one particular example, but rather directs our attention to a variety of groups that derive a centrist identity from their adherence to 'some combination' of the following beliefs and policy orientations:

- Advocacy of change through dialogue and debate rather than violence.
- Support for civil society against the authoritarian state.

- Devaluation of the role of a single figure in favor of collective leadership.
- Enlargement of consciousness that transcends traditional national, sectarian, and other divisions.
- Encouragement of social action with a populist thrust and a broadly social, rather than narrowly religious, cultural or political agenda.
- Bestowal on politics of a sacred character, a spiritual dimension, that expresses itself through the building of the good Islamic community.
- Translation of ethical and religious duties into principles of social responsibility and participation.
- Definition of the sphere of significant social action as both local and transnational.
- Openness to a global dialogue that seriously engages such questions as cultural authenticity, democracy, human rights, and the health of the planet and the welfare of all humankind in the late twentieth century. (Baker in Esposito, 1997: 123)

Although the elements that hold these views to varying degrees are designated centrists (largely due to their commitment to non-violent tactics) many of their aims and practices are radical in that they would entail a serious move towards democratisation by the presently authoritarian Egyptian state.

Baker makes reference to various groupings within this broad tendency, such as the activists working through Egypt's professional syndicates – for example, the Medical and Law Associations, and the al-Shaab group, who were prominent in opposition to the Egyptian Government's unquestioningly pro-American stance in the Gulf War. However, he places particular emphasis on the 'small but enormously creative and outspoken group of religious intellectuals who have organized themselves loosely as a "school," with the aim of providing nonauthoritarian "right guidance" to the various groupings of the Islamic body, including both the al-Shaab and syndicate clusters' (Baker in Esposito, 1997: 125). Baker notes that their ideological stamp is evident in the programme of the *Hizb al-Wasat* (Centre Party), which was set up in the wake of the 1995 elections. Although the *Hizb al-Wasat* is Islamist, having initially taken form as a breakaway movement from the Islamic Brotherhood, it is open enough to include a prominent Egyptian Christian, Rafiq Habib, as one of its chief ideologists. An interview with Habib noted that the

Wasat Party stood for democratisation, religious tolerance, and promotion of women's rights (http://www.cairtimes.com/content/issues/Islists/habib08.html). The party has twice applied for the legal recognition that is required in Egypt for a party to organise lawfully. However, the Shura Council Political Parties Committee, the state body charged with overseeing this process, has turned down their application both times, ostensibly for failing to provide a manifesto that was different from the currently existing parties. This is a catch-all reason that has often been used by the Committee to turn down applications that the Government did not approve of.

What is clear is that the *Hizb al-Wasat* does not resemble the violent fundamentalist movements that are presented as the only face of Islam in the Western media – seemingly a view that is accepted without question by many post-development analysts. In the Egyptian context, the Wasat Party, indeed the *Wassittiyyah*, represent the least exclusionary and violent option for political and social progress.

The phenomenon of Islamic centrism may also be identified in the Turkish Islamic movement of Fethullah Gulen. This movement has been very active in setting up such institutions as high schools, summer camps, universities, and cultural centres, and it has been successful in spreading its ideas widely. Consequently, it has at least influenced a large number of people, with estimates ranging from about 200,000 active supporters to 4 million influenced by Gulen's ideas, which are broadly comparable to those of the *Wassittiyah* in Egypt (Aras and Caha, 2000: 5). He is pro-democratic, arguing that *shari'a* largely pertains to private life and that precepts that concern the state should be interpreted in the context of current realities (Aras and Caha, 2000: 4). Gulen bases his discourse on the contention that Anatolian Islam has always been tolerant and consequently he advocates freedom of worship. He is open to other faiths, and more liberal than other Turkish Islamists on the subject of gender equality, although his views still fall short of being acceptable to modern professional women in Turkey (Aras and Caha, 2000: 4–5).

Against these more liberal aspects of Gulen's movement, it must be noted that it is not internally democratic. Gulen is the unchallenged leader of the movement, which is also characterised by a strict hierarchical structure that is rigidly observed. This seems to be reflected in the fact that the main ideas of the movement seem to emanate from its leader. In addition, we must note that the movement does not take up popular causes that would antagonise the government. In this sense it can only imperfectly represent the genuine day-to-day needs of poorer Turks (Aras and Caha, 2000: 11).

This indicates that Gulen's movement is problematic in a comparable way to COCEI, which was also internally undemocratic. Whereas COCEI combined an exclusory official discourse with emancipatory policies that addressed grass-roots concerns, Gulen's movement has an inclusive discourse, but is quietist at least in terms of its short-run political aims. What can be said is Gulen and his followers are evidently having some success in popularising an Islamism that is non-violent and that seeks to be inclusive, something that has apparently been essentialised out of existence by the post-developmentalists.

5.4   CONCLUSIONS

In this chapter we have seen that the post-development choice of NSMs as a vehicle for popular emancipation is a fortunate one. The activities of groups such as the Zapatistas are evidence of the potential of NSMs to bring about positive change. However, post-development analysis is unable to adequately explain why they are progressive, and why some may be more progressive than others, whilst yet others are not progressive at all. Of course, they favour movements that are emancipatory and that fight exploitation. However, their anti-development stance leads them to define emancipation at least partly in terms of a spurious authenticity. This leads them to accept aspects of their traditional societies that are repressive (as in the case of Rahnema with his dictatorship of the self-defined good, or Esteva and Prakash who overlook the gender inequities of Triqui society) and to reject aspects of modernity that could be of benefit to those at the grass roots (as in the case of Esteva and Prakash who reject modern medicine and education *tout court*). It is notable that this is an error that the Zapatistas avoid in their campaign against traditional gender inequities, not to mention their embrace of modernity in the form of the Internet as a means of propagandising and spreading the struggle.

We may also note that Dagnino (who has collaborated with Arturo Escobar) departs from the discourse of authenticity that seems to be favoured by post-development analysts and uses Gramscian analysis to examine the rise of NSMs and the possibilities for their alliance in an emancipatory project. She is much more successful in this enterprise than any of the post-developmentalists whose conceptualisation of NSMs as a disparate collection of largely unrelated groups protesting against the depredations of modernity does not lend itself to the production of a large-scale strategy. It is worth remembering that Dagnino's Gramscian vision is compatible with Derrida's vision of a New International.

Finally, the post-developmentalists are unable to explain why they exclude certain movements from their elite group of emancipatory NSMs, amongst them Islamist movements. In this chapter we have seen that the criteria for the ideal speech situation and the principle of least violence are far more reliable indicators of the extent to which a group is emancipatory or not. Our analysis of the Zapatistas indicated that their claims to be emancipatory could be supported much more convincingly in terms of such criteria as their refusal of closure and exclusion, rather than by reference to authenticity and an anti-development stance (it is worth noting that the Zapatistas themselves always focus on neo-liberalism as the prime enemy rather than development). Furthermore, our Habermasian and Derridian criteria proved useful in assessing how emancipatory different movements are. We saw that COCEI is more violent and less emancipatory than the Zapatistas in view of the exclusions it makes against women, non-members, and so forth (although observers might still wish to support it for the emancipatory work it does for grass-roots Jucheticos). We were also able to explain why certain groups should be opposed, such as fascist movements that advocate extreme violence. This is a lacuna in post-development theory that leaves them unable to properly explain their condemnation of fascism and which also led them into the mistake of a blanket condemnation of Islamism (thus ignoring various progressive tendencies).

Clearly, the principle of least violence and the criteria underlying the ideal speech situation are much more useful explanatory tools than post-development discourse. They represent a better basis for examining NSMs and their emancipatory nature, or lack of it, and they lend themselves more effectively to the elaboration of a global emancipatory discourse. Moreover, their avoidance of a discourse of authenticity allows for the possibility of grass-roots communities being able to embrace those aspects of modernity that they may see as being of use to them, such as medicine. We may conclude that the principle of least violence and Habermasian discourse theory are developmental in providing a basis for an emancipatory global project based on the activities of NSMs, and also in the sense of allowing for the possibility that the social majorities should be able to embrace those elements of modernity that are of use to them.

6 Aid and the Principle of Least Violence

6.1 INTRODUCTION

We have already seen that post-development analysts regard aid as pernicious in its effects, taking the form of an imposition of disciplinary power by external interests. Escobar typifies such an approach when he refers to development as 'a top-down, ethnocentric, and technocratic approach' that takes the form of 'a system of more or less universally applicable technical interventions', the latter phrase clearly denoting aid programmes and projects. Having classified development aid in this way, he is easily able to move on to his assertion that it 'comes as no surprise that development became a force so destructive to Third World cultures' (see Chapter 2 for the full quotation). The inevitable conclusion that emerges from such an analysis is that Third World people at the grass roots would be better off without aid from the North and that all such interventions should cease.

There is much evidence to discredit what might be termed the mainstream tendency in aid, that which Escobar identifies as the top-down approach. Rondinelli has argued persuasively to the effect that increasingly technocratic approaches to the design of development interventions have been adopted in the attempt by agencies and politicians to maximise efficiency and control. This has happened in the face of increasing evidence to the effect that such aims could only be secured at the expense of flexibility, innovation and adaptability, all qualities that are essential given the complexities and uncertainties attendant on any development intervention. Rondinelli argues as follows:

Systems approaches were introduced not only because they were compatible with macro-economic concepts of development during the 1950s and 1960s, but also because they were perceived as effective methods of reducing uncertainty and increasing the influence of technocrats. Ironically, politicians and administrators embraced control-oriented planning and management techniques that were either ineffective, or inherently incapable of reducing uncertainty at a time when the recognition that development was an uncertain process was becoming widespread. (Rondinelli, 1983: 5)

Indeed, most agencies insist on rigorously planned projects, often backed up by statistical exercises such as cost-benefit analysis to demonstrate the profitability of the proposed project. As Rondinelli notes, such exercises are hopelessly abstract, reflecting little about the values and needs of the interest groups involved in the project (for a full critique of such techniques see Rondinelli, 1983: 15–22). They also effectively move any control of the project away from those it directly affects to a group of remote experts who have the skill to perform these complex, but dubiously relevant exercises.

Such is the essence of top-down bureaucracy. Any significant decisions concerning project objectives, design and implementation are taken by experts rather than those that the project directly affects. The result is that the aid recipients, those that the project is supposedly for, often feel that a project has been imposed on them with little concern for their needs as they see them. It is hardly surprising then that they generally feel little sense of ownership of the project, taking few if any pains to preserve it when the aid donor withdraws from the scene. Clearly, such an approach is not conducive to project success or sustainability. Moreover, Escobar is quite correct to condemn such interventions as disciplinary impositions of alien power and aims on people at the grass roots.

Quite apart from the distortions of aid arising out of the politico-bureaucratic power centres that administer much aid, one must recognise that large elements of aid funding are compromised by politico-diplomatic considerations. These usually manifest themselves in ways that are inimical to the aid having any beneficial effects on the ground. One manifestation takes the form of continuing to give aid to repressive and corrupt rulers because they adopt the political position required by the donor. Burnell comments on this in the following terms:

For many years DAC aid and US aid in particular was intended to perform the express functions of stabilizing pro-Western governments, containing the spread of communism and limiting the expansion of Soviet influence. Among many such governments with close US ties were a significant number of personal and military dictatorships with poor human rights records, for instance the Somoza dynasty in Nicaragua from the 1930s to 1979. An even larger number were exceedingly corrupt, including the Marcos presidency in the Phillipines (1965–86) ... Governments who seemed inclined towards substantial redistributive policies, or friendship with the USSR, were penalized. They found their loan applications to multilateral development banks obstructed, and in many cases bilateral support was provided to their political opponents such as the military in Chile's democratically elected government headed by President Allende (1970–3), a professed Marxist ... Here, aid's immediate objective was not stability but the political destabilization of incumbent regimes. Instability was judged instrumental to the interrelated purposes of projecting US hegemony and safeguarding capitalism worldwide. (Burnell, 1997: 105)

That such political considerations remain salient in the aftermath of the Cold War is demonstrated by the continuation of US aid on a grand scale to Egypt. It would seem that the Mubarak Government's relatively tolerant stance towards Israel more than compensates for its dubious human rights record and its corruption. Some European states have also been known to show preferences for client states that have a penchant for human rights (and other) abuses. Thus, the United Kingdom is thought to have prevented the suspension of European Union aid to Kenya under the terms of the Lome Convention, despite the Moi Government's political repression, whilst France is reputed to have protected Togo from suspension of its EU aid despite the brutal nature of the Eyedama Government.

Many aid donors are known to relax their criteria for the acceptance of aid projects in cases where they particularly want to develop a favourable relationship with a specific state. Such an example is provided by World Bank support of Indonesia's disastrous Transmigration Project. The official rationale for this project was to relieve population pressure in Java and Bali by relocating some 140 million people from these islands to the outer islands in the Indonesian archipelago. A more covert reason was to promote Javanisation of the outer islands in order to enhance government control over areas where its writ was only dubiously observed. The project was ill-conceived in various respects. It left out of account the infertility of the soils on the islands and the interests of the existing population who lived through light farming, hunting and fishing. Even so, the Bank supported the project because its then president, Robert McNamara, 'wanted to work with Suharto, and this was Suharto's pet project' (World Bank official quoted in Caufield, 1996: 118). The Bank lent over US$1 billion for the project over the period of the 1970s and 1980s, a period when the project caused the deforestation of huge areas of virgin rainforest in order to provide land for the influx of migrants from Java. Large numbers of indigenous forest dwellers were uprooted from their traditional homes in the forest without compensation, whilst many of the settlers were allocated hopelessly infertile land from which they were unable to make an adequate living. The Bank supported this environmental and human disaster because McNamara wanted to enhance its position in the Third World by striking up a friendship with Suharto (details of the Transmigration Project are taken from Caufield, 1996: 117–120).

These variegated distortions of development aid have led a variety of observers ranging across the political spectrum from left to right, to reject aid as a pernicious influence on the well-being of Third World people. The post-development analysts generally seem to gravitate around a position that only movements that have spontaneously arisen from the grass roots can be seen as emancipatory. Such a position clearly implies that an external intervention such as provision of aid by a Northern agency cannot result in any form of development (construed as emancipatory change) for those living at the grass roots in the South.

However, this raises important questions for external forces that are sympathetic to a project of emancipation for people at the grass roots. Should such forces refrain from all intervention, leaving the task of emancipation to Southern grass-roots movements and organisations? What of situations where such organisations do not exist? Should the poor and oppressed be left to organise themselves or starve? The latter situation is clearly unacceptable under a principle of least violence. To stand aside in a situation where people are left in a state of poverty is to aquiesce and accept their deprivation. It is violent. A further impetus towards intervention may be derived from the arguments of theorists such as Freire, who wrote:

Self-depreciation is a characteristic of the oppressed, which derives from their internalization of the opinion the oppressors hold of them. So often do they hear that they are good for nothing and are incapable of learning anything – that they are sick, lazy and unproductive – that in the end they become convinced of their own unfitness. (Freire quoted in Burkey, 1993: 51)

Freire argues that the Southern poor often have too little confidence to make their own initiatives, and the more powerful social forces in the South have little interest in helping them, often because they are actively engaged in exploiting the poor. If such situations of injustice are to be corrected change must be initiated from the outside and this often means by Northern agencies.

Such initiatives depart from the models of aid criticised above, these being aid as an over-complex intervention controlled from the top down, and aid as a political bribe to Southern elite groups. The writings of analysts such as Freire, Rahman, Oakley and Burkey have led to the genesis of a new strategy that avoids such pitfalls, this being 'self-reliant participatory development'. In brief, this strategy involves a development worker (known variously as a 'change agent', an 'animator', or 'project agent') working with groups in a community on projects that those groups have identified and developed themselves. The change agent's role is not like that of the traditional expert, who imparts (an often incomprehensible) wisdom and leaves. Instead s/he is supposed to live with the community for a period, gradually building trust with local people, and then engaging them in a dialogue with the object of prompting them to think how they might change their own lives for the better. This refers to the process of 'conscientisation' through which local people become self-reliant and are empowered in the sense that they gain confidence to make their own initiatives.

In the rest of this chapter we shall examine participatory development with a view to establishing how far it goes towards providing an aid strategy that may be deemed ethically acceptable. In particular we shall assess how far it accords with the criterion of taking the path of least violence.

6.2   PARTICIPATION AS A DEVELOPMENT OF LEAST VIOLENCE

A variety of definitions of participation have been offered. Oakley gathered together the following:

(a) Participation is considered a voluntary contribution by the people in one or another of the public programmes supposed to contribute to national development, but the people are not expected to take part in shaping the programme or criticizing its contents. (Economic Commission for Latin America, 1973)

(b) With regard to rural development ... participation includes people's involvement in decision-making processes, in implementing programmes, their sharing in the benefits of development programmes and their involvement in efforts to evaluate such programmes. (Cohen and Uphoff, 1977)

(c) Participation is concerned with ... the organized efforts to increase control over resources and regulative institutions in given social situations on the part of groups and movements of those hitherto excluded from such control. (Pearse and Stiefel, 1979)

(d) Community participation [is] an active process by which beneficiary or client groups influence the direction and execution of a development project with a view to enhancing their well-being in terms of income, personal growth, self-reliance or other values they cherish. (Paul, 1987, quoted in Oakley, 1991: 6)

While these definitions of participation are not mutually exclusive, it would be fair to say that statements (a) and (c) represent radically different approaches. The first statement is suggestive that people are mobilised to volunteer some work on a project without actually having any substantive voice in determining what it will do and how it will do it. However, statement (c) makes it clear that those hitherto excluded are to be given a measure of control. Statement (c) entails empowerment, whereas (a) does not.

This is linked to the question of whether participation is considered as a means that is used to achieve project objectives, or as an end in its own right. It should be clear that participation used purely as a means is simply a variant on traditional top-down development. In statement (a) the people are mobilised to do externally directed work on externally decided project objectives. They are not empowered in any sense. However, participation as an end includes a clear emancipatory moment inasmuch as organisation and empowerment have increasingly been identified as central aspects of participation as an end. Oakley notes that the World Conference on Agrarian Reform and Rural Development (WCARRD) 'emphasised the importance of a transfer of power as implicit in participation' in 1979, since which time empowerment has come to be an accepted term in the development world (Oakley, 1991: 9). Authors like

Oakley emphasise that participation can be very helpful in building a sense of project ownership in beneficiary groups, which can have beneficial knock-on effects in terms of enhancing project efficiency, effectiveness, and sustainability (Oakley, 1991: 117–18). However, our central interest in participation is in its efficacy for bringing about emancipation for those at the grass roots.

How then does participatory development work and in what sense can it be seen as bringing about emancipation? As we have already noted, it often (if not usually) has to be started by an external agency. Oakley points out that whilst groups have emerged spontaneously in some areas, notably India and Latin America, 'more commonly an external agency takes the first step in initiating the process' (1991: 175). Usually the first step will involve sending one, or possibly two change agents to work in a community. Burkey cautions us against attempts to work with a whole community, noting that even small rural villages will be characterised by social differentiation between different interest groups, particularly those who are better off and those who are worse off. Relations between these groups may well be characterised by exploitation. Burkey notes that the Community Development Movement that started in India in 1952 assumed the existence of a rural social solidarity, only to find that the richer members of the rural communities were using their influence to appropriate the lion's share of any benefits from the movement's programmes. Burkey draws the conclusion that account must be taken of the differential interests of variant sectors of the community in identifying a group to work with. Only through developing such an understanding of the community can the change agent discover which groups are most in need of aid. Furthermore, it is often best to work (at least initially) with a group characterised by broadly common interests, as this militates against tendencies towards disagreements as to what the group's central aims should be. (See Burkey, 1993, chapter 3 for a fuller explication of these issues.)

The central method of commencing the participatory process is Participatory Action Research (PAR). According to Burkey, the 'preliminary objectives of PAR should be: (1) to increase the development worker's understanding of the local situation; and (2) to increase the insight of the local people, especially the poor, into what factors and relationships are the root causes of, and contributing factors to, their poverty' (Burkey, 1993: 60). In this way the change agent learns about the social structure, different interests, and variant problems of the community, whilst local people are prompted and encouraged to analyse their own problems, thus generating local knowledge on which action can be based. PAR is based on the dialogic approach, which Burkey describes as consisting of 'an interchange and discussion of ideas based on a process of open and frank questioning and analysis in both directions between the investigators and the people, both individually and in small groups' (Burkey, 1993: 62). Rahman places emphasis on the way in which traditional research is constituted in such a way as to generate a subject–object relationship between the proactive researcher and those who are researched and regarded as inert matter that is acted on (Rahman, 1993: 89). A central element in PAR is that it should eliminate the distinction between change agent and community, or group member, thus collapsing the subject–object relationship. Rahman elaborates on this to the effect that:

> For participatory action, by the people, the people must develop their own knowledge. This is not to suggest intellectual autarky for the people; but one must stand on one's own knowledge to be able to trade with others' knowledge as equals; only then can one participate rather than becoming dominated. (Rahman in Burkey, 1993: 63)

This means that a group that has been engaged in such a dialogue with a change agent is liberated from the normal passive role of aid recipient, and is encouraged to generate its own analysis of its situation and what to do about it. The element of praxis is central to PAR. Comstock and Fox assert:

> The validity of the results of participatory research can be gauged first, by the extent to which the new knowledge can be used to inform collective action and second, by the degree to which a community moves towards the practice of a self-sustaining process of democratic learning and liberating action. (in Burkey, 1993: 63–4)

In other words, the process is not a finite one in which people analyse a particular problem and act to solve it. Action prompts further analysis, which leads on to more action. It is worth noting in passing how closely this resembles Derrida's analysis of decision-making, in which any decision inevitably makes exclusions that return to haunt the decision, thus necessitating another decision. Similarly, Comstock and Fox clearly understand that the process of emancipation cannot be reduced to a singular event, be it a project or a revolution. Rather, it is a continuous process of analysis and action to emancipate the excluded.

Obviously, the fact that this process is initiated by a change agent puts considerable pressure on the performer of this role. It might well be argued that a natural tendency would be for the change agent to become a leader, taking a central role in the discussion of problems, their definition, and formulation of strategies to solve them. Clearly, such action would be to fall into the trap of acting as an over-determined and determining subject, dominating his or her grass-roots constituency rather than empowering them. Naturally, the theorists of participation are aware of such dangers and have attempted to define the change agent's proper role. Oakley characterises the various dimensions of the change agent's role as follows:

Animation: A process of assisting rural people to develop their own intellectual capacities, that is, to stimulate their critical awareness; this critical awareness enables rural people to examine and explain issues in their own words and, as a result to realize what they can do to bring about change.

Structuring: The development of internal cohesion and solidarity among rural people, and of some form of structure or organization which can help bring the people together and serve as a forum for their continued involvement.

Facilitation: A service role which assists rural people to undertake specific actions designed to strengthen their participation; these actions can include the acquiring of particular technical skills, gaining access to available resources or translating their own ideas into feasible projects.

Intermediary: To serve, in the initial stages, as a go-between in relation to other external services or forces; to help establish contacts with existing services and introduce rural people to the procedures and mechanisms for dealing with these services.

Linking: To help develop links between rural people in similar contexts and facing similar problems; this

Withdrawal: linking at district and regional level creates a wider base of support for participation.

A progressive redundancy, whereby the agent consciously withdraws from a direct role with the people and increasingly encourages them to undertake and manage the projects in which they are involved. (Oakley, 1991: 182)

Burkey uses the comments of a number of experienced activists to elaborate on the change agent's role in various ways. It is noted that 'change agents should work *with* the people and not *for* them because people have to be the subjects and not the objects or targets of change'. They should also 'work mainly with vulnerable groups who have benefited the least or have actually been harmed by previous developmental efforts'. Burkey characterises the animation, or conscientisation phase as follows:

The most important role of change agents is to *initiate a process of critical awareness building* (conscientisation) among the rural poor. They should set in motion a dialogue on the realities of the local situation and so enable the people to identify their own needs and problems and express what kind of changes they want, how they would like to see them come about. It was emphasized that change agents should not impose their own ideas on the people. The process of identifying problems and finding solutions is extremely important, and the people, not the change agents, must determine the pace and direction of this process. Economy of time or effort should be no argument for change agents to impose their own views and ideologies on the people. (Burkey, 1993: 79)

Burkey continues to note that change agents should '*assist the people to appreciate the advantages of working in groups*, because it is only through group action that the poor stand a chance of increasing their bargaining power and control over their own lives' (Burkey, 1993: 79). However, they should not become the main impetus behind group formation since genuine commitment to the group can only come from the people themselves. Without such commitment group activities are unlikely to be sustained. Burkey also stresses the need for change agents to share their skills and outside linkages with the people, but in a way that is not demeaning. They should also seek to develop and encourage leadership skills within their groups, as well as monitoring their own performance to ensure that they are not lapsing into the trap of becoming leaders themselves. Perhaps Burkey's key statement as to the role of the change agent is the following:

Change agents have to realize that genuine people's organizations and movements have to start as people's movements. It is the people themselves who must be the driving force of a movement from the beginning. In fact it cannot be otherwise. Activity initiated and led by outsiders might appear impressive for some time, but eventually one would find that this was a deceptive appearance. Increased and continuous participation of the people has to be regarded not just as a means of achieving certain ends, but also as an end in itself. It is the participation of the people that will act as an internal safeguard against new oppressive vested interests which might emerge from inside the new organizations. (Burkey, 1993: 80)

It should be clear from all this that although the change agent may provide the initial impetus towards a group coming together to discuss their mutual problems, it is the people who are motivated to analyse their problems, organise to address them, plan activities to solve them, and put those activities into action. The change agent serves only as a facilitator in the latter phases of the process. Burkey stresses that 'decisions must be taken by the participants themselves', since '[m]aking decisions, even wrong ones, from the very beginning of the group's life is essential for establishing a continuing self-reliant development process' (Burkey, 1993: 151).

Stress is also laid on the process through which the change agent initially makes contact in a community. Burkey notes that local acceptance of a change agent can only be won gradually through living with a community for a sufficient period to gain their confidence (Burkey, 1993: 78). In order to win local confidence, the change agent should proceed patiently and respectfully, demonstrating a willingness to learn from the local community. The agent should also live to a standard not too dissimilar from that of the group s/he hopes to work with. In this way the agent may gain local knowledge of the community and its problems, whilst also coming to be accepted as somebody that is trustworthy. Oakley cites the example of a female change agent working in Brazil who spent a year observing some fisherwomen before one of them took the initiative and made contact with her. Several further contacts with various fisherwomen led to the formation of groups that conducted some successful welfare activities (Oakley, 1991: 171). Through allowing the community time to get used to her and to realise that she meant them no harm, the change agent was able to facilitate formation of a group that brought about some positive change for the fisherwomen.

That change agents themselves are aware of the delicacy of their role is demonstrated by the comments of activists when asked about common weaknesses amongst change agents. Amongst the problems that they pointed out was the tendency for agents to become pater-nalistic, treating people like children, and to do everything themselves, not allowing the people to gain experience of working for their own self-defined goals (Burkey, 1993: 83). It should be clear then that participatory methodology is aimed at generating a self-aware and self-reliant movement of the people rather than one that is reliant on external leadership, resources and plans.

One might ask how far it works. A central case study that is often cited in works on participation is that of Sarilakas in the Phillipines. Sarilakas was the successor to Project Aid, a nominally participatory project that was actually a top-down intervention. Project Aid set up a number of groups in various areas, promising to deliver loans and various other resources to them. A large number of these promises were broken and consequently many of the groups were inactive by 1981 when Sarilakas took over. The orientation of Sarilakas was to build up people's capacities for organisation through providing education and training on such matters as management and technical skills where appropriate (Haarland in Oakley, 1991: 101). Each group's activities would be decided by the group membership rather than the facilitator, and a deliberate policy of gradually withdrawing the facilitator was followed in order to avoid group dependency.

The types of activities undertaken by Sarilakas groups may be illus-trated with reference to the following examples. Firstly, Barangay Amar Farmer's Association set up their own collective savings fund in 1981 so that they would not be forced to deal with exploitative moneylenders or the Land Bank. They also purchased a hand-tractor, which some members needed because they did not have a bullock and plough. A revolving fund was created on the basis of a loan that the change agents negotiated with the Canadian Government. By late 1982 the group was sufficiently successful to be able to buy a rice mill since there were none nearby and to build a warehouse where they kept the mill, the tractor and their rice (Rahman, 1993: 53–4). A second example can be drawn from Barangay Taludtod, a sugar producing area, where landless labourers and tenant producers are exploited by big landlords who control the transport to the sugar mill. In 1975 the landlords nearly doubled the fee for transporting cane to the mill, a situation that still pertained in 1981 when two Sarilakas change agents arrived in the area. They revived the group that had been set up by Project Aid and helped it to mount a legal challenge to the landlords, which eventually resulted in a substantial reduction of the transport fee. The group also began a rice distribution project so that all the members could buy their rice needs at once rather than individually, enabling them to obtain a cheaper and more certain supply (Rahman, 1993: 57–9). On the basis of such examples Rahman concludes:

> Under Project AID the promises of the project staff kept the people alienated from their own capabilities and strength to tackle their own issues and achieve their rights. The SARILAKAS facilitators behaved differently. They integrated with the people, and stimulated them to deliberate on what they could do themselves. The educational seminars raised the people's awareness of their rights. Armed with this knowledge and stimulated to take initiatives themselves, the people deliberated and took action which ranged from the purely economic to full 'pressure group' activities to assert and achieve their rights as rural workers. (Rahman, 1993: 59)

In this case aid actually helped people at the grass roots to form their own democratic movements in order to take emancipatory action.

One can point to many other examples of successful participatory development including case studies gathered in the work of analysts like Burkey, Oakley and Rahman. For our purposes it is worth paying a little more attention to a forestry project financed by Australia in Nepal, the Nepal–Australia Forestry Project (NAFP), because this particular venture illustrates a learning experience on the part of the managers of NAFP as to how participatory techniques could be used to bring about change more effectively than traditional top-down methods. NAFP started in 1979 with the objective of creating new forested areas, which would help to stabilise the environment and provide needs for the local community such as fuelwood. In the first instance the project was a typical top-down venture with aims and activities defined by specialists and little consideration being given to involving local people who used the forest. However, it was realised that the new forested areas were insignificant compared with the forest areas being used by the local populace. It was decided that degradation of these larger areas could be prevented by a strategy that drew the local forest users into the sustainable management of the forest. Consequently, the project called a meeting in Tukucha, an area with several forest boundaries around it. The meeting consisted of local community leaders and men, and it set up a committee which turned out to be ineffective at least partly because it did not understand what it was supposed to do. Further meetings were called and committees set up before it was realised that the meetings had only succeeded in mobilising local notables and men. They had not reached the poor and women who were amongst the most significant of the forest users. This led to the formation of a committee in which the various sectors of the community were represented. Despite some conflict between the better-off and the poor a number of decisions were taken concerning such issues as 'the regulation of leaf collection and firewood cutting, the organization of labour to cut a fireline in the forest, and the planting of a small area of degraded land' (Hobley in Oakley, 1991: 114). A new role was also developed for forest rangers, which involved working with villagers, 'identifying the forest users, listening to problems, stimulating discussion, helping to resolve conflicts and finally bringing together the forest users to manage the forest collectively' (Hobley, in Oakley, 1991: 115). There were some doubts as to how sustainable the participatory approach of NAFP would prove to be given that the project did not challenge existing inequalities in forest rights between the powerful members of local communities and the poor. Participation by the poor might be expected to decline in the face of evidence that the main benefits of the project were going to the wealthier members of the community. Even so, it was clear that the project was more effective when at least some account was taken of the interests of the poor and they were included in the committees that were entrusted with the management of the forest.

It may reasonably be argued that this example provides at least partial confirmation for the utility of the Habermasian model of the ideal speech situation and of the principle of least violence. When NAFP moved to bring the poor into the process of decision-making on how best to manage the forests, the project became more effective both in terms of preservation of the forest and meeting the needs of the generality of forest users. That these were only partial gains may be attributed to the fact that, although the poor were included in deliberations, they were at least partially silenced inasmuch as they were not allowed to challenge the interests of the powerful forest users. In this sense the project falls short of reaching the conditions for an ideal speech situation, a failure that endangers its goal of creating a sustainable system for managing the forests to the benefit of the majority of those making their living from the forest. Similarly, the gains made when NAFP became more participatory may be presented as the resultant of bringing in those who were excluded, a clear step onto a path of less violence than the exclusory top-down model that the project had first adopted. This logic would suggest the desirability (if not ethical obligation) of taking a step further in the empowerment of the poor, that of facilitating them in challenging social relations through which they are exploited or otherwise disadvantaged. By contrast with this a post-development analyst would simply dismiss all aid as pernicious, thus defining out of existence any benefits gained by the Nepalese forest dwellers from NAFP, as well as the undoubted benefits that were gained by many Filipinos through the activities of Sarilakas.

In fact a post-development critique of participation has been mounted by Rahnema. The starting point for this critique is that where there is oppression local people are aware of it and resist it. Change agents simply impose their own conceptions of mobilisation and political action 'dis-valuing the traditional and vernacular forms of power' (Rahnema in Sachs, 1992: 123). But how can Rahnema be sure that effective resistance arises in all such situations? Many of the strategies that he refers to, such as tax evasion, are individuated responses to oppression. They may provide some relief for the individual practising them. However, such tactics are unlikely to be effective in the sense of bringing about any social change that will end the oppressive situation, unless they are organised on a wider scale, for example as a tax boycott. If we accept that effective organisation is unlikely to take place in every conceivable situation of repression, it follows that Rahnema's dismissal of external intervention amounts to an abandonment of those communities that are unable to organise. It seems ethically untenable to argue that such groups should be left to endure their oppression, especially when we can point to Sarilakas and numerous other case studies to provide examples of people being mobilised to improve their situation through participatory techniques. By contrast, one can point to the example of the indigenous forest dwellers expelled from their homes in the forest by Indonesia's transmigration programme. Many of them became members of the urban unemployed in the absence of any effective resistance to their forced removal (organised either internally or externally). It is also worth remembering that the Zapatistas did not arise spontaneously out of the Lacondan Jungle, but were initially stimulated by a core group of Marxist guerrillas who took refuge there in 1983 to escape from the state repression of the time (Lorenzano in Holloway and Pelaez, 1998: 127). The significance of the Zapatista experience is that this core group listened to the local people and learned from them just as change agents are supposed to. In a sense their experience paralleled that of participation. The guerrillas provided the initial spark for activity, but did not impose their own models for action, instead learning from local models and combining the two in a successful fusion of popular power.

Rahnema goes on to argue how many change agents end up dominating their groups imposing their ideologies and definitions on the people. Apart from his failure to acknowledge the fact that this is recognised as an ever-present danger by participatory organisations, Rahnema provides no evidence to counter the many examples cited by Burkey, Rahman and Oakley to the effect that: first, not all change agents behave in this way and that, secondly, there are clear instances of participation succeeding in mobilising self-reliant groups.

Rahnema proceeds by focusing on Freire's rationale for conscientisation to the effect that many people at the grass roots have not achieved a 'critical consciousness' that enables them to critique and reject the value positions and discourses of dominant and exploiting classes (in Sachs, 1992: 125). Rahnema concedes that Freire is correct on this point, itself a position that is difficult to reconcile with his earlier assertion that the people will always resist oppression. However, he goes on from this basis to argue that change agents do not apply the principle to themselves in terms of undertaking a self-criticism of their own ideological positions. This leads to a repetition of the accusation that change agents impose their own values on people. He refers to 'the many cases where highly ideologized "agents of change" or "vanguards", have tried to use conscientization or participatory methods, simply as new and more subtle forms of manipulation' (Rahnema in Sachs, 1992: 125). As we have seen, the sort of indoctrination that Rahnema is referring to is anathema to participatory technique, which emphasises the need for outsiders to learn from the people rather than imposing their own views.

Undoubtedly, there are some change agents who abuse their positions to try and impose their views on the groups that they work with. However, this is not universal and it cannot be taken as completely discrediting participation unless Rahnema has an alternative that eliminates this risk. However, all that he has to offer is the insight that participation should be based on a spiritual dimension that helps revive 'the old ideals of a livelihood based on love, conviviality and simplicity, and also in helping people to resist the disruptive effects of economization' (Rahnema in Sachs, 1992: 127). This sense of participation 'implies, above all, the recovery of one's inner freedom, that is, to learn to listen and to share, free from any fear or predefined conclusion, belief or judgment' (Rahnema in Sachs, 1992: 127). He concludes that '[i]f the participatory ideal could, in simple terms, be redefined by such qualities as attention, sensitivity, goodness or compassion, and supported by such regenerative acts as learning, relating and listening, are not these qualities and gifts precisely impossible to co-opt?' (Rahnema in Sachs, 1992: 129). Yet the latter qualities are precisely what the dialogic method attempts to achieve, and commentators like Burkey, Rahman and Oakley provide practical advice on how to achieve them and how to avoid imposition of the change agent's own views. Moreover, their advice is based on experience that has been successfully tested in the field. All that Rahnema has to offer by contrast is a vague admonition to incorporate a spiritual dimension into development work. This is a worthy nostrum, but it tells us precisely nothing about how to help those who are in need of it.

6.3   CONCLUSIONS

In this chapter we have shown that not all aid has to represent an imposition of power on people at the grass roots. Development initiatives that take participation as an end in itself can actually help to mobilise the oppressed and the poorest in development projects that they have defined themselves. That these projects are emancipatory is indicated by the actions of those involved who have felt sufficiently empowered to change their environments and to improve their living standards.

None of this is to detract from those Southern movements like Chipko that have arisen out of the activities of grass-roots people.

However, it does indicate that in those instances where the oppressed have not been able to organise themselves there is an ethical justification for an aid intervention to assist them in achieving the self-reliance to mobilise in pursuit of their own self-defined objectives. Indeed, it could be argued that the omission of such an intervention would be ethically unacceptable in that it would entail tolerance of the current situation of poverty and oppression. It would be the course of greater violence, abandoning the excluded to their current oppressed status. Participatory bottom-up development can therefore be identified as constituting part of a development of least violence.

We can see then that the principle of least violence yet again provides a more utile and ethical guide to action than a post-development position. The latter view would lead to a proscription of all aid as a necessarily harmful intervention, implicitly leaving many of the oppressed to suffer. By contrast, the principle of least violence helps us to identify an aid strategy that nuances intervention in such a way as to minimise its harm, while facilitating a process through which the poor can begin to define and work towards their own development.

7   Conclusion

It may have occurred to the reader that the title of this book, *The End of Development*, is a play on words. It plays on the sense of the word, 'end', as a finish, or closure, and its sense as an objective. A number of post-development theorists feel that the objectives of development have become hopelessly confused, obscured, and corrupted, and that consequently the enterprise of development should be brought to a close. By contrast, this book has argued that such a closure would be precipitate, indeed violent. It has argued for a reconfiguration of the concept of development in accordance with a Derridian approach.

As we noted at the beginning of this book, the post-development approach tends to regard the continual changes that have manifested themselves in the concept of development as a sign of that concept's growing amorphousness and irrelevance. The need to keep adding new elements to the concept of development, such as gender and sustainability, are signs of the concept's continuing inadequacy, leading many post-development analysts to advocate its abandonment. The Derridian approach outlined in Chapter 4 would suggest that the myriad new approaches that have been incorporated under the rubric of development are indeed a sign of the continued inadequacy of that concept, but that this is also a sign of its continued relevance. Rather than being a sign of the redundancy of 'development', such change is a sign of the continuing necessity for the concept of development. These changes indicate that our formulations of development inevitably make exclusions that subsequently demand the revision of said formulations to take account of what has been repressed or omitted. This does not reflect development's irrelevance, but rather the continued demand for development by those that are excluded. What does this tell us about development? Certainly, it does not suggest that development is finished as a project. Development is likely to continue for as long as there are groups of the excluded that wish to pursue their own projects for development.

However, this Derridian approach does throw doubt on development cast in the form of metatheory. The proclivity to formulate

160

development as a teleological progress towards some ultimate form of society itself practises violent closure. The attempt to programme the perfect society, whether it be capitalist or communist, communitarian or individualist, will inevitably exclude by defining certain forces or groupings out of existence. Such is a course of maximum violence. However, this does not discredit development. In the same way that Derrida advocates a de-ontologised Marxism, a Marxism stripped of an eschatological progress towards communism, we can conceive of a development that does not lead to an essentialised ultimate developed society. In this sense also development has no end. It is a project without a horizon.

One might ask if development is worth pursuing if it is precisely that which cannot be obtained. Why engage in development activity if the incompleteness of our formulations makes development itself so elusive? A deconstructionist response would suggest that we are ethically obliged to do so. To the extent that our own theories, dicta, and concepts are exclusory, or oppressive, we have an obligation to the excluded, the obligation to work with them against their oppression and exclusion. Any proposition that there will always be the oppressed and the excluded does not in any way negate our obligations towards those that we have excluded. One must also question any assumption that a project will be invalidated by its failure to achieve a perfect outcome. Is the democratic project invalidated by humanity's manifest failure to produce a perfectly inclusive society? Surely not. It is always possible for a society to become more democratic and inclusive even if 'perfect democracy' must remain an unobtainable horizon. Similarly, we can argue of development that beneficial changes can be achieved (for example in health and education) even if a perfect or complete development must remain unachievable. This suggests that, not only is development a project without a horizon, but also a project that we are morally obliged to participate in, and one that can achieve worthwhile, although not ultimate or absolute results. Development is far from at an end in terms of being finished.

Against such arguments post-development analysts are likely to protest that all too often the effects of development are deleterious and exclusory rather than beneficial. At this stage it should be clear that violence is not of itself any reason for approbation or disapprobation. Violence is inevitable. A more salient question pertains to the amount of violence that is caused by our actions. Do we take the course of least violence, or do we maximise violence? Either path can be taken, this being the central question that ethics puts to us. We can accept or refuse an ethical obligation to minimise violence. Accordingly, some developmentalists endeavour to follow the course of least violence while others refuse it. We have already seen how Derrida criticised neo-liberalism for its exclusions, while championing Marxism for its defining gesture of openness to the oppressed and excluded. Similarly, we may critique neo-liberal and capitalist approaches to development because of their violent exclusion of the poor and all those who do not readily fit into the vision of the free market *nirvana*. However, this leaves open the course of endorsing and backing development projects that seek to promote inclusion of the oppressed. This is a much more nuanced approach than that taken by many of the post-development analysts, of dismissing development altogether and advocating their own post-development projects, many of which are themselves exclusory, implying a course of greater violence.

This line of argument brings us to the second sense of the word 'end' in that it touches on questions concerning objectives, bringing into play the issue of what development is for. To the extent that development has no horizon it should be clear that the objective(s) of development cannot take the form of some essentialised goal of history, whether it be communism, or the mass, high-consumer society envisaged by Rostow, or free-market capitalism. Indeed, the absence of a horizon infers that no complete or finalised account of the objectives of development can be given. However, this does not mean that we can give no account of development. The logic of the Derridian approach expounded here indicates that development must entail the emancipation of excluded or oppressed groups. To put it slightly differently it implies the right of social and other groups to pursue their own projects for the good life – with the proviso that such groups observe the principle of least violence themselves.

Another way in which we can try to identify objectives of development is to turn our attention to issues of process, and to elaborate the conditions required for a developmental process. In response to post-development analysts who used Foucaultian discourse theory to critique the mobilisation of disciplinary power effected by development discourse, we used Habermasian discourse theory to try and establish a basis for a democratic and egalitarian discourse. The Habermasian 'ideal speech situation' as recast by Blaug offers a model for a discourse that is explicitly designed with a view to avoiding conditions in which any group can be repressed. Such a context would provide conditions in which variant groups would be able to enunciate and pursue their own projects. As we have seen, the central reservation over such a project concerns Habermas' tendency to assume a telos of consensus in human communication. A number of critics suggest that this assumption tends to efface difference. Indeed, the model of the ISS does imply that decisions and outcomes can be attained that will be universally agreeable (if not actually satisfactory) and to the extent that this is the case it imposes closure. We have argued that this can be corrected for by observing the principle of least violence, which would mean that such discourses could not be seen as leading to any absolute decision or resolution. All such outcomes of discourse would be subject to continual re-examination and revision. A central contention of this book is that such a process provides a viable process in which development can be pursued.

The development approach advocated here has a number of analytical advantages over the post-development theories examined in this book. The relativist stance embraced by many of the post-development analysts leaves them unable to determine whether or not particular groups and projects are emancipatory. We have already seen that they wanted to condemn some groups as unemancipatory (hence the blanket condemnation of fundamentalisms), but their relativism left them unable to explain why the projects of some groups might be deemed objectionable whilst others were acceptable. As was demonstrated in Chapter 5, the principle of least violence provides us with an analytical tool through which we can examine how emancipatory various groups or projects are. For example, we could see that the Zapatistas are clearly more emancipatory than COCEI (as examined by Rubin) in that they maintain an open project that avoids closure, whereas COCEI defines its project largely in terms of worker emancipation, which tends to elide over very real elements of gender oppression. In addition, the ISS provides a reference point through which we can compare how far the respective organisations follow democratic/participatory processes. Again, the difference between the bottom-up participation practised by the EZLN and the centralised policy-making process of COCEI was made obvious by reference to the ISS. Use of these analytical tools also enabled us to establish that Islamism should not necessarily be subjected to the knee-jerk dismissal administered by many of the post-development analysts. In all these respects the concept of development advanced here is more analytically nuanced than the post-development approach.

This approach to development also avoids a problem of political quietism implicit in post-development analysis. We have noted that the post-development critique implies that external forces should not intervene in the efforts of Southern peoples to pursue their own projects. According to this view all aid is to be avoided as an external imposition of power. Whilst it must be acknowledged that much of what passes for aid is neo-imperialist, or harmful in other senses, this author would argue that the position of eliminating all aid is violent in that it deprives many of the poor at the grass roots of the opportunity to receive resources that could be of practical help to them. Yet again, we saw in Chapter 6 that the principle of least violence and the ISS provide us with the analytical tools to determine which aid interventions are harmful, as against those which are more participatory, motivating and assisting local communities in the pursuit of their own projects.

We may conclude by observing that development is not at an end. It cannot come to an end, because its ends (objectives) must undergo a process of constant redefinition, and this will last as long as there are groups that pursue their own projects of emancipation. Given the elusiveness of the developed, or perfectly inclusive society, it seems likely that such groups will continue to emerge for the foreseeable future. The future of development and its manifold objectives will continue to unfold with their emergence.

Bibliography

Alvarez, Sonia, Dagnino, Evelina, and Escobar, Arturo (eds), *Cultures of Politics/Politics of Cultures: Re-Visioning Latin American Social Movements.* (Boulder: Westview Press, 1998).

Alvarez, Sonia, Dagnino, Evelina, and Escobar, Arturo, 'Introduction: The Cultural and the Political in Latin American Social Movements', in Alvarez, Dagnino and Escobar (eds), *Cultures of Politics/Politics of Cultures: Re-Visioning Latin American Social Movements.* (Boulder: Westview Press, 1998).

An-Naim, Abdullahi Ahmed, *Toward an Islamic Reformation.* (Syracuse: Syracuse University Press, 1990).

Appignanesi, Lisa, *Postmodernism: ICA Documents.* (London: Free Association Books, 1989).

Aras, Bulent and Caha, Omer, 'Fethullah Gulen and his Liberal "Turkish Islam" Movement', *Middle East Review of International Affairs.* Vol. 4, No. 4 (December 2000).

Arkoun, Mohammed, trans. Robert D. Lee, *Rethinking Islam: Common Questions Uncommon Answers.* (Boulder: Westview, 1994).

Baker, Raymond, 'Invidious Comparisons: Realism, Postmodern Globalism, and Centrist Islamic Movements in Egypt' in Esposito, John, *Political Islam: Revolution, Radicalism, or Reform?* (Boulder: Lynne Rienner, 1997).

Bauman, Z., *Postmodern Ethics.* (Oxford: Blackwell, 1993).

Beardsworth, Richard, *Derrida & the Political.* (London: Routledge, 1996).

Benhabib, S. *Critique, Norm and Utopia.* (New York: Columbia University Press, 1986).

Bennington, Geoffrey, *Interrupting Derrida.* (London: Routledge, 2000).

Blaug, Ricardo, *Democracy: Real and Ideal.* (Albany: State University of New York Press, 1999).

Burkey, Stan, *People First: A Guide to Self-Reliant, Participatory Rural Development.* (London: Zed Books, 1993).

Burnell, Peter, *Foreign Aid in a Changing World.* (Buckingham: Open University Press, 1997).

Caufield, Catherine, *Masters of Illusion: The World Bank and the Poverty of Nations.* (London: Pan Books, 1996).

Cecena, Ana Esther, and Barreda, Andres, 'Chiapas and the Global Restructuring of Capital' in Holloway, John and Pelaez, Eloina (eds), *Zapatista!* (London: Pluto Press, 1998).

Chambers, Robert, *Rural Development: Putting the Last First.* (Harlow: Longman, 1983).

Clarkson, Linda, Morrissette, Vern, and Regallet, Gabriel, 'Our Responsibility to the Seventh Generation' in Rahnema, M. and Bawtree, V. (eds), *The Post Development Reader.* (London: Zed Books, 1997).

Cohen, J.N. and Uphoff, N., *Rural Development Participation: Concepts and Measures for Project Design Implementation and Evaluation*. (Ithaca, N.Y. Cornell University, 1977).

Cowen, M.P. and Shenton, R.W., *Doctrines of Development*. (London: Routledge, 1996).

Critchley, Simon, *The Ethics of Deconstruction: Derrida and Levinas*. (Oxford: Blackwell, 1992).

Crush, Jonathan, *Power of Development*. (London: Routledge, 1995).

Dagnino, Evelina, 'Culture, Citizenship, and Democracy: Changing Discourses and Practices of the Latin American Left' in Alvarez, Sonia, Dagnino, Evelina, and Escobar, Arturo (eds), *Cultures of Politics/Politics of Cultures: Re-Visioning Latin American Social Movements*. (Boulder: Westview Press, 1998).

Dahl, Gudrun, and Megerssa, Gemetchu, 'The Spiral of the Ram's Horn: Boran Concepts of Development' in Rahnema, M. and Bawtree, V. (eds), *The Post Development Reader*. (London: Zed Books, 1997).

Derrida, Jacques, *Of Grammatology*, trans. Gayatri Spivak. (Baltimore: Johns Hopkins University Press, 1976).

Derrida, Jacques, *Writing and Difference*, trans. Alan Bass. (London: Routledge and Kegan Paul, 1978).

Derrida, Jacques, *Dissemination*, trans. Barbara Johnson. (Chicago: University of Chicago Press, 1981).

Derrida, Jacques, *Margins of Philosophy*, trans. Alan Bass. (Chicago: University of Chicago Press, 1982).

Derrida, Jacques, *Limited Inc*, trans. Samuel Weber. (Evanston: Northwestern University Press, 1988).

Derrida, Jacques, *Of Spirit: Heidegger and the Question*, trans. Geoffrey Bennington and Rachel Bowlby. (Chicago: University of Chicago Press, 1989).

Derrida, Jacques, *Specters of Marx: The State of the Debt, the Work of Mourning and the New International*, trans. Peggy Kamuf. (London: Routledge, 1994).

Derrida, Jacques, 'Remarks on Deconstruction and Pragmatism', trans. Simon Critchley, in Mouffe, Chantal (ed.), *Deconstruction and Pragmatism*. (London: Routledge, 1996).

Derrida, Jacques, *The Politics of Friendship*, trans. George Collins. (London: Verso, 1997).

Derrida, Jacques, *Adieu to Emmanuel Levinas*, trans. Pascale-Anne Brault and Michael Naas. (Stanford: Stanford University Press, 1999).

Derrida, Jacques, 'Marx & Sons', trans. G.M. Goshgarian, in Sprinker, Michael (ed.), *Ghostly Demarcations*. (London: Verso, 1999).

Dronsfield, J. and Midgley, N. (eds), *Responsibilities of Deconstruction*. (Warwick: Warwick Journal of Philosophy, 1997).

Dupré, Louis, *Passage to Modernity: An Essay in the Hermeneutics of Nature and Culture*. (New Haven: Yale University Press, 1993).

Economic Commission for Latin America, 'Popular participation in development', in *Community Development Journal* (Oxford), Vol. 8, No. 2, 1973: pp. 77–93.

Escobar, Arturo, *Encountering Development: The Making and Unmaking of the Third World*. (Princeton: Princeton University Press, 1995).

Esteva, Gustavo, 'Development' in Sachs, W. (ed.), *The Development Dictionary: A Guide to Knowledge as Power*. (London: Zed Press, 1992).

Esteva, Gustavo and Prakash, Madhu Suri, *Grassroots Post-Modernism: Remaking the Soil of Cultures*. (London: Zed Books, 1998).

Esteva, Gustavo and Prakash, Madhu Suri, 'Beyond development, what?', *Development in Practice*, Vol. 8, No. 3 (August 1998).

Flacks, Richard, 'The Party's Over – So What Is to Be Done?', in Larana, Enrique, Johnston, Hank, and Gusfield, Joseph (eds), *New Social Movements*. (Philadelphia: Temple University Press, 1994).

Flynn, Thomas, 'Foucault's mapping of history', in Gutting, Gary (ed.), *Cambridge Companion to Foucault*. (Cambridge: Cambridge University Press, 1994).

Foucault, Michel, *Madness and Civilization*, trans. Richard Howard. (New York: Pantheon, 1965).

Foucault, Michel, *The Order of Things*, trans. Alan Sheridan. (New York: Random House, 1970).

Foucault, Michel, *The Archaeology of Knowledge*, trans. Alan Sheridan. (New York: Pantheon, 1972).

Foucault, Michel, *The Birth of the Clinic*, trans. Alan Sheridan. (New York: Vintage, 1973).

Foucault, Michel, *The History of Sexuality*, Vol. 1: 'An Introduction', trans. R. Hurley. (New York: Pantheon, 1978).

Foucault, Michel, *Discipline and Punish*, trans. Alan Sheridan. (New York: Vintage, 1979).

Foucault, Michel, 'The Use of Pleasure', *The History of Sexuality*, Vol. 2, trans. R. Hurley. (New York: Pantheon, 1985).

Foucault, Michel, 'The Care of the Self', *The History of Sexuality*, Vol. 2, trans. R. Hurley. (New York: Pantheon, 1986).

Fraser, Nancy, 'Foucault on Modern Power: Empirical Insights and Normative Confusions', *Praxis International* 1(3), 1981: 272–87.

Grueso, Libia, Rosero, Carlos, and Escobar, Arturo, 'The Process of Black Community Organizing in the Southern Pacific Coast Region of Colombia' in Alvarez, Sonia, Dagnino, Evelina, and Escobar, Arturo (eds), *Cultures of Politics/Politics of Cultures: Re-Visioning Latin American Social Movements*. (Boulder: Westview Press, 1998).

Gutting, Gary (ed.), *Cambridge Companion to Foucault*. (Cambridge: Cambridge University Press, 1994).

Habermas, Jurgen, *The Theory of Communicative Action. Vol. 1. Reason and the Rationalisation of Society*, trans. Thomas McCarthy. (Boston: Beacon Press, 1984).

Habermas, Jurgen, *The Theory of Communicative Action. Vol. 2. Lifeworld and System: A Critique of Functionalist Reason*, trans. Thomas McCarthy. (Boston: Beacon Press, 1987).

Habermas, Jurgen, *The Philosophical Discourse of Modernity: Twelve Lectures*, trans. Frederick Lawrence. (Cambridge, Mass: MIT Press, 1987).

Habermas, Jurgen, *Moral Consciousness and Communicative Action*. (Cambridge: Polity Press, 1990).

Habermas, Jurgen, *Postmetaphysical Thinking*, trans. William Mark Hohengarten. (Cambridge: Polity Press, 1992).

Habib, Rafiq, (http://www.cairtimes.com/content/issues/Islists/habib08.html)

Hand, Sean (ed.), *The Levinas Reader*. (Oxford: Blackwell, 1989).

Held, David, *Introduction to Critical Theory: Horkheimer to Habermas*. (Cambridge: Polity Press, 1980).

Heller, Agnes, *A Theory of Modernity*. (Oxford: Blackwell, 1999).

Hobson, Marian, *Jacques Derrida: Opening Lines*. (London: Routledge, 1998).

Holloway, John, 'Dignity's Revolt' in Holloway and Pelaez (eds), *Zapatista!* (London: Pluto Press, 1998).

Holloway, John and Pelaez, Eloina, *Zapatista!* (London: Pluto Press, 1998).

Holloway, John and Pelaez, Eloina, 'Introduction: Reinventing Revolution', in Holloway and Pelaez (eds), *Zapatista!* (London: Pluto Press, 1998).

Honderich, Ted, *The Oxford Companion to Philosophy*. (Oxford: Oxford University Press, 1995).

Johnston, Hank, Larana, Enrique, and Gusfield, Joseph R., 'Identities, Grievances, and New Social Movements', in Larana, Enrique, Johnston, Hank, and Gusfield, Joseph (eds), *New Social Movements*. (Philadelphia: Temple University Press, 1994).

Larana, Enrique, Johnston, Hank, and Gusfield, Joseph (eds), *New Social Movements*. (Philadelphia: Temple University Press, 1994).

Lee, Robert D., *Overcoming Tradition and Modernity: The Search for Islamic Authenticity*. (Boulder: Westview, 1997).

Levinas, Emmanuel, *Otherwise than Being or Beyond Essence*. (The Hague: Martinus Nijhoff, 1981).

Levinas, Emmanuel, *Ethics and Infinity: Conversations with Philippe Nemo*, trans. R.A. Cohen (Pittsburgh: Duquesne University Press, 1985).

Lorenzano, Luis, 'Zapatismo: Recomposition of Labour, Radical Democracy and Revolutionary Project' in Holloway, John and Pelaez, Eloina, *Zapatista!* (London: Pluto Press, 1998).

Lyotard, Jean-Francois, *The Postmodern Condition*. (Minneapolis: University of Minnesota Press, 1984).

Lyotard, Jean-Francois, 'What is Postmodernism?' (Appendix to *The Postmodern Condition*. Minneapolis: University of Minnesota Press, 1984).

May, Todd, *Reconsidering Difference*. (University Park: University of Pennsylvania, 1997).

Melucci, Alberto, 'Social Movements, Culture and Democracy', *Development and Change*, Vol. 23, No. 3, July 1992.

Millan, Margara, 'Zapatista Indigenous Women' in Holloway, John and Pelaez, Eloina (eds), *Zapatista!* (London: Pluto Press, 1998).

Moss, Jeremy, *The Later Foucault*. (London: SAGE Publications, 1998).

Mouffe, Chantal (ed.), *Deconstruction and Pragmatism*. (London: Routledge, 1996).

Norberg-Hodge, Helena, 'Learning from Ladakh', in Rahnema, Majid and Bawtree, Victoria, *The Post Development Reader*. (London: Zed Books, 1997).

Norris, C., 'Interview with Jacques Derrida', in A. Papadakis *et al.* (eds), *Deconstruction: Omnibus Volume*. (London: Academy Editions, 1989).

Norris, C., '"What is Enlightenment?": Kant and Foucault' in Gutting, Gary (ed.), *Cambridge Companion to Foucault*. (Cambridge: Cambridge University Press, 1994).

Oakley, Peter, Bortei-Doku, Ellen, Therlrildsen, Ole, Sanders, David, Harland, Charlotte, Garibay, Adriana Herrera and UNIFEM, *Projects with People*. (Geneva: International Labour Organization, 1991).

Paul, S. *Community Participation in Development Projects*, Discussion Paper No. 6. (Washington DC: World Bank, 1987).

Pearse, A. and Stiefel, M. *Inquiry into Participation*. (Geneva: UNRISD, 1979).

Pippin, Robert, *Modernism as a Philosophical Problem*. 2nd edn. (Oxford: Blackwell Publishers, 1991).

Porter, Doug, 'Scenes From Childhood: The homesickness of development discourses', in Crush, Jonathan (ed.), *Power of Development*. (London: Routledge, 1995).

Rabinow, Paul, 'Modern and countermodern: Ethos and epoch in Heidegger and Foucault', in Gutting, Gary (ed.), *Cambridge Companion to Foucault*. (Cambridge: Cambridge University Press, 1994).

Rahman, Md Anisur, *People's Self Development*. (London: Zed Books, 1993).

Rahnema, Majid, 'Participation', in Sachs, W. (ed.), *The Development Dictionary: A Guide to Knowledge as Power*. (London: Zed Press, 1992).

Rahnema, Majid, 'Afterword: Towards Post-Development: Searching for Signposts, A New Language and New Paradigms', in Rahnema, Majid and Bawtree, Victoria (eds), *The Post Development Reader*. (London: Zed Books, 1997).

Rahnema, Majid and Bawtree, Victoria (eds), *The Post Development Reader*. (London: Zed Books, 1997).

Rondinelli, Dennis, *Development Projects As Policy Experiments: An Adaptive Approach to Development Administration*. (London: Methuen, 1983).

Rorty, Richard, 'Habermas and Lyotard on Postmodernity', in Bernstein, R. (ed.), *Habermas and Modernity*. (Cambridge: Polity Press, 1985).

Rouse, Joseph, 'Power/Knowledge', in Gutting, Gary (ed.), *Cambridge Companion to Foucault*. (Cambridge: Cambridge University Press, 1994).

Rubin, Jeffrey, 'Ambiguity and Contradiction in a Radical Popular Movement' in Alvarez, Sonia, Dagnino, Evelina, and Escobar, Arturo (eds), *Cultures of Politics/Politics of Cultures: Re-Visioning Latin American Social Movements*. (Boulder: Westview Press, 1998).

Ryan, M., *Marxism and Deconstruction: A Critical Articulation*. (Baltimore: Johns Hopkins University Press, 1982).

Sachs, W. (ed.), *The Development Dictionary: A Guide to Knowledge as Power*. (London: Zed Press, 1992).

Sarup, Madan, *Post Structuralism and Post Modernism*. (New York: Harvester Wheatsheaf, 1988).

Schuurman, Frans J. (ed.), *Beyond the Impasse*. (London: Zed Books, 1993).

Sidahmed, Abdel Salam and Ehteshami, Anoushirvan, *Islamic Fundamentalism*. (Boulder: Westview Press, 1996).

Simons, Jon, *Foucault & the Political*. (London: Routledge, 1995).

Smart, Barry, 'Foucault, Levinas and the Subject of Responsibility' in Moss, Jeremy (ed.), *The Later Foucault*. (London: SAGE Publications, 1998).

Sprinker, Michael (ed.), *Ghostly Demarcations*. (London: Verso, 1999).

Tarnas, Richard, *The Passion of the Western Mind*. (London: Pimlico, 1991).

Visker, Rudi, *Michel Foucault: Genealogy as Critique*, trans. Chris Turner. (London: Verso, 1995).

Warnke, Georgia, 'Communicative rationality and cultural values', in White, Stephen K. (ed.), *The Cambridge Companion to Habermas*. (Cambridge: Cambridge University Press, 1995).

Warren, Mark E., 'The self in discursive democracy', in White, Stephen K. (ed.), *The Cambridge Companion to Habermas*. (Cambridge: Cambridge University Press, 1995).

Wellmer. Albrecht, 'On the Dialectic of Modernism and Postmodernism', *Praxis International*, **4**, 1985.

White, Stephen, 'Foucault's Challenge to Critical Theory', *American Political Science Review*, **80**(2) 1986: 419–32.

White, Stephen K. (ed.), *The Cambridge Companion to Habermas*. (Cambridge: Cambridge University Press, 1995).

Wright, T., Hayes, P. and Ainley, A., 'The Paradox of Morality: an Interview with Emmanuel Levinas', in R. Bernasconi and D. Wood (eds), *The Provocation of Levinas: Rethinking the Other*. (London: Routledge, 1988).

The Concise Routledge Encyclopaedia of Philosophy. (London: Routledge, 2000).

Index

Compiled by Sue Carlton